Journey of the Heart

Finding Healing After Loss

JoAnne Chitwood

Border Mountain Books

Border Mountain Books
An Imprint of Promise Productions
PO Box 870593
Wasilla, AK 99687

Printed in the United States of America

Notice: This book is not intended to take the place of professional mental health care. It is offered with no guarantee on the part of the author or Promise Productions. The author and publisher disclaim all liability in connection with the use of this book.

To David
my brother
a "broken soul made whole"

I will see you again

Journey of the Heart
Finding Healing After Loss

This study manual is designed as a workbook for both groups and individuals working through the grief of a significant loss. If you are not working with a grief recovery group, strongly consider finding a trusted friend that you can share the group exercises with. Being able to honestly verbalize your thoughts and feelings is an important part of the healing process.

1. Understanding Loss
Examining the Ways that Loss is a Wound

"Just the facts, please…"

   The surgeon makes a skillful cut across the man's chest, revealing layers of muscle, tissue, and bone. He performs an intricate cardiac operation, then carefully stitches the parts together again. The patient spends days and even weeks experiencing acute pain from the operation. Although he was an active mountain climber before the surgery, he puts off his upcoming climb until the next year, knowing he'll need time for his body to heal and his heart to recover from the trauma of the surgery.

   Even a year after the procedure, when the scar has healed to a pink line and the doctors have given him a clean bill of health, the man continues to feel the reminders of his trauma. Occasionally, searing pain in the scar area lets him know that damaged nerves have not yet recovered.

   A loss can affect human emotions in much the same way the surgeon's knife impacts the body. Any kind of a loss creates an emotional wound. The more serious the loss to the individual, the more severe the wound will be. And, just as a physical wound takes months and sometimes years to heal, so healing from an emotional wound takes time.

   Because emotional wounds leave no visible scars, our society is less tolerant of the need for healing time. Comments like, "It's been six months since her husband died and she's still crying. She's going to have to pull herself together," are far too common. The impatience with which those who are grieving are sometimes treated only serves to increase their feeling of brokenness, isolation, and despair.

   Someone once said, "Grief is not a problem to be solved. It is simply a statement that you have loved someone." The pain of separation is love's price tag and those who have had the courage to love deeply in spite of the potential pain of loss, deserve support through the difficult days of the healing process.

Some questions you may be asking…

 Can grief be cumulative? It seems that all my losses have piled up on me at once.

The answer is a resounding "yes". Loss is a part of life, from birth to death. In our very mobile society today, loss is much more a part of life than it has ever been. Many of us no longer live in extended families with predictable futures as farmers or shepherds or keepers of vineyards—lifestyles that are rooted in the earth and produce a deep stability. We move a lot. Our children may leave us for distant lands and their own fast paced careers.

Illness, loss of long cherished goals, the loss of youth, beauty, or strength that accompanies the aging process, the loss of a job through retirement, being laid off or fired… all are losses that accumulate through the years. Each loss must be grieved for healing to occur. But all too often, the grief process is stifled and emotions are "stuffed". Then, when a huge loss such as the death of a loved one occurs, all those unresolved grief issues surface along with the pain of the new loss. It can feel very overwhelming.

 My emotions seem all jumbled up and I'm afraid that if I start crying, I'll never stop. Is there any rhyme or reason to this nightmare? How long do these feelings last?

It is normal to have many conflicting emotions when you have experienced a major loss. You may be going along "just fine" when suddenly a certain odor or a song on the radio reminds you of your loss and your feelings take you right back to a very painful place. You may feel that your mind is "out to get you" because it will bring up memories and painful thoughts when all you may want is to get way from the pain and never feel it again.

*What your mind, thoughts, and emotions are doing when they bring those painful thoughts around is just what they need to do to help you heal. The only way **OUT** of the pain that accompanies loss is to go **THROUGH** the pain. You will find, as you gradually heal, that you will be able to take longer and longer glimpses at what you have lost until you come to a place of acceptance. You may cry a lot in the process. It may even feel that the tears will never stop, but they eventually will. Tears are healing and cleanse the body of toxins. Let them flow.*

There IS a general pattern to the grief process, although every individual is unique and your experience with grief will be different in some ways than anyone else's. It often helps to know, however, what to expect as far as some of the basic characteristics of the human grief response.

*Grief counselors often find that it is helpful to look at the grief process in terms of five stages: **Denial, anger, bargaining, depression,** and **acceptance**. At times the grieving person will find themselves reverting back to the earlier stages in the grief process without warning or any particular reason that they can see. Understanding that **this is normal** and to be expected can help allay some of the panicky feelings that this disturbing experience can cause. Let's look at what you may experience as you move through these stages:*

1. Shock

Shock, denial, a feeling of numbness—these are the first reactions of the body when it experiences a severe emotional assault. We can't believe or comprehend what has happened to us. Life feels like a bad dream that we're sure we're going to wake up from and everything will be as it was before the loss occurred. Sometimes, we actually forget that it has happened and we find ourselves stunned as we are confronted with the truth again.

2. Emotional Upheaval

When the shock begins to wear off, it can be very distressing to discover that underlying strong emotion as such as intense anger, fear, remorse, and extreme loneliness are beginning to wreak havoc with our lives. We may begin to realize how much we depended upon the person we have lost and feel the loss acutely. These feelings can lead to a loss of self-esteem and feelings of inadequacy.

3. Depression

As feelings of anger, fear, and loneliness intensify, feelings of helplessness and hopelessness are often added. It is not uncommon for someone who is in this most uncomfortable phase of the grief process to long for death himself as a release from the pain.

4. Physical Symptoms

Don't be surprised if you find yourself developing the same physical symptoms as your loved one (if they died after an illness). Some other physical signs of grieving are irritability and

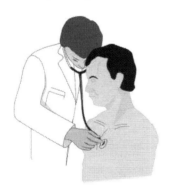

restlessness, inability to sleep chest pain and muscle aches, low energy level, loss of appetite, shallow breathing, hyperventilation, changes in speech patterns, and difficulty concentrating. Be patient with yourself when these physical symptoms occur. They will gradually lessen as healing occurs.

5. Anxiety

During this stage, you may fear losing the memory of your loved one. You may have vivid dreams, while awake or asleep, in which you "see" your loved one, perhaps calling out to you for help or acknowledgment. This can be a very frightening and disturbing experience.

6. Hostility

About six weeks after the loss of your loved one, you may experience a period of rage. You may be confused and frightened by the intensity of your anger and see it as inappropriate, but feel unable to defuse it. Some people, in an attempt to keep their loved ones from seeing their anger, may turn their rage inward in self-abusive ways.

7. Guilt

"Should" is a favorite word of someone experiencing this phase of the grief process. "I should have stopped to see him that day" or "I shouldn't have yelled at her about cleaning her room before she left" are common statements. Death has a way of amplifying whatever issues existed between the deceased and the survivor before the death occurred. Problems that seemed insignificant while your loved one was still alive may become major obstacles to your peace of mind now.

8. Fear

You may experience fear in many forms during this time: fear of being alone in the house where your loved one died, fear of going out, fear of any new relationships no matter what their nature, fear of never being happy again, fear of being happy and feeling guilty about it, or fear of waking up in the morning and feeling the pain of being so alone.

9. Memory Healing

During this phase of bereavement, memories both good and bad ebb and flow through your mind. It is usually easier to process the bad memories first, because in many ways, the good memories are the most painful to recall.

10. Acceptance

Accepting the reality of your loved one's death and forgetting them are two different things. As with the healing of any serious wound, a scar will always remain to remind you of the injury. You will never be the same, because loving and losing someone special changes you forever. Although acceptance and "letting go" usually take one or two years to achieve, 100% healing never happens.

"Loss is loss, no matter what the cause. When someone or something we love is taken from us or denied us, that is a loss... The greater our loss- the more intensely we feel each of the stages of recovery- the longer it takes to pass from one stage to another. With small losses, the stages of recovery can be moved through in minutes. For large losses, it can take years."

From *How to Survive the Loss of a Love,* Colgrove, Bloomfield and McWilliams.

 Are there any general guidelines as to what to expect at certain times after the loss?

No two people will go through the grief process in exactly the same way and no time schedule will fit everyone's experience. There are, however, some general guidelines that can help in understanding where you might be in your healing process. They have been called the "critical time intervals".

First 48 Hours

The shock from the death can be intense during this time and the emotions frightening. Denial may be very strong during the first few hours.

First Week

Many of the actions during this time are automatic: funeral planning, calling relatives, taking care of business. This time of gathering strength to do what has to be done may be followed by a time of emotional and physical exhaustion.

Second to Fifth Weeks

This time period may be characterized by a feeling of abandonment as friends and family members return to their normal routines after the funeral. If you are trying to maintain a job at this time, your employer may expect you to be fully recovered and functional at work. You may even feel as if you can be fully functional as some residual denial my be still insulating you from the full impact of the loss. You may find yourself saying things like, "Well, it's not as bad as I thought it would be. I can handle this."

Sixth to Twelfth Weeks

It's during this time that the anesthetic of denial may wear completely off and the reality of the loss hits with full force. Some of the things you may experience during this time are:

- Sleep changes
- Unpredictable bouts of crying
- Onset of fear, sometimes paranoia
- Wanting to "punish" something or someone for your pain
- Changes in sexual desire/activity
- Inability to concentrate
- Fatigue and generalized weakness
- Muscle tremors
- Loss of motivation
- Extreme mood swings
- Change in appetite
- Desire for isolation
- Need to talk about the deceased
- Physical symptoms of distress, such as shortness of breath or chest pain

Third to Fourth Month

As the nightmare drags on, there is a decreased tolerance towards frustration. A cycle of "good days" and "bad days" develops. It is during this time that the immune system takes the hardest hit and colds and flu have a heyday with your system, adding their discomfort to the pain of just making it from day to day.

Six Months

This milestone can be excruciatingly painful, resurrecting all the events of the loss and starting the cycle of emotional upheaval all over again (although for a shorter time). This reaction is also common during holidays, birthdays, and other special occasions.

Twelve Months

The first anniversary of the death can be very difficult. The painful time usually lasts about a week (most of it in the days preceding the day). If you have been able to work through your grief during the year leading up to the anniversary date, this could also mark the beginning of emotional resolution for you.

Eighteen to Twenty-four Months

This is the time that resolution often occurs. The raw pain has healed and you may be able to bear the pain of the separation enough to proceed with your life. There is an emotional "letting go" that occurs when you no longer use the death as the focal point around which the rest of your life revolves (although it will probably always be a major reference point).

At the Heart of the Matter

Use the space below to write something about your loss. Who was the person you lost or the situation that caused your grief? What made this person special to you, if your loss was a relationship through death, divorce, or a break-up of some kind? In what ways has your life been affected by this loss? If you feel comfortable doing so, share something with the group about your "wound".

What physical signs of grief have you experienced? What emotional signs? In what ways have these affected your day-to-day life?

Read the following poem, then write one of your own, expressing your feelings about the loss that has occurred in your life. If you feel comfortable doing so, share your poem with the group.

Brother

I walked around a corner today,
Thought I saw you.

Your jaunty cap just so.
Flash of plaid.
Vice grip around my heart.

Who knew that heart-ache isn't
Just a figure of speech?

JoAnne Chitwood

_____

_____

_____

_____

_____

_____

_____

_____

Putting It Into Practice

One of the most important things you can do for yourself when wounded by a major loss is to take care of yourself in very special ways. Society acknowledges the need to rest and recover after surgery. The patient is expected to spend several months recovering from the physical trauma he has experienced under the surgeon's knife.

Your loved ones and friends may not realize that you need extended recovery time from the emotional wound of a loss. It's okay to gently remind them of your needs.

Here are some suggested actions to incorporate into your daily routine to help you deal with the stress of your loss. Review them as a group and choose one or two to begin to incorporate into your life this week.

Find a place all your own where you can go, undisturbed, every day. Use the solitude to relax, meditate and pray, and regroup.

Learn to accept comforting words from others. Practice affirming yourself using positive self-talk. The healing energy that is generated when positive words are spoken is essential for emotional and spiritual well-being whatever the circumstances. And especially now, in the raw pain of your loss, you can find warmth and comfort in the healing cycle of giving and receiving love and affirmation.

In the initial stages of grief, it is difficult to make decisions. Indeed, as we will explore later, it is best not to make any major decisions for a year or so after a serious loss.

It is important, even when faced with small decisions, to remind yourself that you are not a victim of circumstances, no matter how difficult they may seem. Make it a point to say, "I choose to..." rather than "I should...". Say "I won't..." rather than "I can't...". Your choice of words will be a continual reminder to your battered heart that your freedom of choice is still intact.

Establish a "buddy system". Use it regularly as a source of encouragement, support, and re-direction. Nothing is more valuable than a trusted friend who will not only accept us and comfort us, but who will also gently tell us the truth about our behavior patterns.

Open your eyes to the beauty and joy that still exists around you in spite of the ache in your heart. Each day, express gratitude for at least five things in your life that you are thankful for. It seems too simple to be true, but gratitude is one of the most potent emotional healers known to man.

Take a few minutes now to create a "care plan" for yourself this week. Write down some ways you plan to nurture yourself. Include any changes you may need to make in the way you relate to your own needs. If you feel comfortable doing so, share your care plan with the group.

Resilience

A major factor in how you respond to traumatic events in your life (and this major loss you are experiencing is a trauma to your heart and mind) is your level of resilience. Resilience isn't really something you can quantify and if you haven't previously had a traumatic event happen in your life, you may not know whether you are resilient or not. The dictionary defines personal resilience as the capacity to recover quickly from difficulties. How does this capacity develop? What makes the difference between someone who responds with resilience to life's tragedies and heartaches and one who is flattened by them?

Research shows that we can make ourselves more or less vulnerable to being traumatized by tragedy and loss by the way we think about things. The stories we tell ourselves have a major impact on how resilient we are in the face of difficulty. And, whether we realize it or not, we tell ourselves stories every day about what is happening to us and what it means. We may engage in patterns of worrying about minor things, blowing them up and creating a crisis out of them. Some people call this "awfulizing" or "catastrophizing". If we choose this approach to problems on a day-to-day basis, we create neural pathways in our brain that become habit. Then, when it comes to a major life event, our brain naturally goes to the negative and we don't have effective skills in coping with what is happening. We feel as if we have no control over our circumstances and feelings and we are being tossed around by cruel outward forces. And the reality is, the more inflexible we are the more we will be negatively affected by traumatic events.

Or we may choose a different path. When difficulties come, we may choose to face them, learn from them, and grow. We still tell ourselves a story about what is happening to us, but it is a story that focuses on what can be learned from the circumstances and how we can make the situation better for ourselves and for others. Instead of focusing on what we can't control and feeling victimized, we choose to look for the hidden gifts in what is happening. We feel the grief as we pass through the stages and we also remind ourselves that it will not feel like this forever.

Resilience can be learned, even in later life. Helpful therapies like Cognitive Behavioral Therapy, EMDR, Internal Family Systems Therapy, and Emotional Freedom Technique (tapping) can teach us to:
  • Reframe a situation in our minds, changing it from a negative slant to a more positive one
  • Shift our energy charge from highly emotional to more calm and rational
  • Change the center of control from external circumstances to internal, giving us a sense of personal power, even in the middle of pain and difficulty
  • Pull back from broad globalizing of the trauma to looking at specific aspects we can influence
  • Change our perspective from seeing the problem as permanent to reminding ourselves that it is "not forever" and "this too shall pass"

The pain of loss is real. Resilience doesn't take away our grief. It does, however, provide a way to move through the bereavement process and come out the other side transformed by our grief, instead of crushed. It opens us up to love in a new way, with a deeper understanding of life and a renewed sense of being part of the human family.

A Closer Look

During this time of upheaval and pain, it's difficult to imagine any of the craziness of grief as being "normal". There is a difference, however, between a grief process in which your heart is gradually healing and one in which you are stuck and need extra help to get over the hump.

The following list identifies signs that could indicate an unhealthy grief process. Remember that the line between "healthy' and "unhealthy" grief can often be very thin and sometimes indistinguishable. It is the degree of intensity or the length of time a certain symptom persists, rather than the symptom's presence that is important.

- **Avoiding any thoughts or feelings about the loss**

- **Significant preoccupation with the death or loss many months after its occurrence**

- **Large memory gaps**

- **Flashbacks, hallucinations, and nightmares**

- **A continuing, significant disinterest in the activities of daily life**

- **"Worshiping" and over-idealizing the person who died, so much so that it interferes with daily life even months after the death**

- **Severe irritability and outbursts of anger toward others in the family and toward coworkers**

- **Feeling out of control and unable to cope for an extended period of time**

- Using alcohol and/or drugs to keep from experiencing the pain of the grief process

- Avoiding all relationships for fear another loss will occur

- Flat affect—no emotion at all, even after the first few weeks following the loss

- Continuing tension and insomnia that isn't relieved with relaxation techniques

- Ongoing physical symptoms such as heart palpitations, severe startle reflexes, cold sweats, and breathing difficulties

- The development of new problems sleeping, eating or relaxing that weren't occurring previously

- Ongoing, persistent feelings of guilt for surviving when the loved one died

- Talking about suicide, especially if a plan is formulated

"Grief is not a problem to be solved. It is simply a statement that you have loved someone."

Author Unknown

In the following space, write your feelings and thoughts about the statement above.

2. Nature's Anesthetic

A Closer Look at Shock and Denial and How to Cope

"Just the facts, please..."

The surgeon steps close to the patient to begin his work. As skilled as he is, he wouldn't even consider making that first incision until the patient is properly anesthetized. The shock and denial phase in the grief process is as necessary when an emotional wound has occurred as the anesthetic is in a surgical procedure.

Major loss assaults the emotions and the impact can be overwhelming. A total nervous breakdown could very well occur as a result were it not for the softening, distracting effect of denial. Family members and friends may be concerned during this phase that the grieving one isn't "facing reality". They may bring the "facts" of the loss to the griever's attention, trying to get them to acknowledge the "truth" and make decisions concerning the future.

The *truth* is: the mind will accept the loss as it is ready to. While the griever consciously denies the reality of the loss to some extent, his subconscious is busily at work preparing him for the pain of full acknowledgment.

There is a well-known story in Judeo-Christian tradition that tells of a man who had a dream. In the dream he saw footprints in the sand of his life. One set belonged to him and the other set to God. He noticed that in times of grief and loss that there was only one set of footprints and he asked God why he had been left alone during his most difficult times. God replied that the man had never been left alone at all—but those times when there was only one set of prints were the times that God carried him.

And that is exactly what happens during the shock and denial phase of grief. While it is impossible to believe or comprehend what has happened, while the mind refuses to accept a reality too painful to face, while the body's natural protection against intense pain is still fully activated—this is the time that the grieving person is "carried". There is nothing to fix, no reality to impose, no reason to fear the denial. The shock will dissipate soon enough. It is important to let it be and allow it to do it's work.

Some questions you may be asking...

 How can I know if I'm in the denial phase of grief if my mind is "denying" it?

It isn't the actual grief process that the mind is denying during this stage. Shock and denial are not synonymous with amnesia. It is the loss itself that the mind denies and even this is usually on a feeling level. Some common reactions are:

- *How could this happen to me?*

- *My life feels like a nightmare. I keep thinking I'm going to wake up and it will all have been just a bad dream.*

- *I don't feel anything at all. Just numb. If I loved her so much, why don't I feel it?*

- *I wake up in the morning and, for a few seconds, I forget that my life will never be the same again. Then I remember, and it seems so unreal, like it's happening to someone else.*

- *I've been on autopilot. There are things to be done and I do them. But sometimes I drive all the way across town and when I get there, I can't remember any of the trip. No stoplights, no turns, no landmarks... It's scary.*

 If part of my brain is "turned off", isn't it dangerous for me to be making decisions and trying to function "normally"?

Yes. And again I say, YES. This is an especially vulnerable time in your life. That is why it is of utmost importance NOT to make important decisions at this point. This is not the time to put on a brave front and pretend that you "have it all together" even if the numbness of denial gives the illusion that it might be true.

Even when the earlier phase of shock and denial gives way to the other stages of grief, shock and denial can take over again at any point when the body feels unable to cope with the emotional strain of the loss. There is no safe time in the first year or so of the grief process to make major decisions.

Hopefully, you have a safe support system in place to which you can turn at this time for guidance and directions. It's not easy to "need" others in many cultures, so it may feel awkward and unnatural to ask for help. But it is okay. All of us take a turn in that seat sooner or later, and your experience there will help you to be a more sensitive "support provider" in the future.

Don't expect others to be able to read your mind and know what you need. Even though you may not know what you need sometimes, don't hesitate to speak your mind when you do. Here are some examples of asking for help:

"I'm exhausted and can't even think about what to eat for dinner, much less fill out these Medicare papers. Will you help me with them?"

"Would you come over and sit with me for an hour this afternoon? The house seems so empty."

"I would love to have lunch with you and talk. Just hearing your voice is comforting to me. Would tomorrow work for you?"

"I need help deciding what to do with his things. Would you be willing to give me a hand with them?"

Things to Avoid
(in the first year following a major loss)

- Beginning a new romantic relationship
- Buying or selling a house
- Changing jobs or careers
- Adopting a new baby
- Moving to another area of the country
- Getting a new pet
- Making any major financial decisions
- Extensive travel
- Any kind of gambling, drugs, or alcohol

What are some of the physical and emotional symptoms that I can expect?

Physical symptoms that occur in response to major loss are very similar to those of a post traumatic stress disorder victim. In many ways, major loss is as traumatic as being in a war zone. Some things to watch for are:

- *Sleeplessness*
- *Irritability*
- *Emotional "numbness"*
- *Difficulty concentrating*
- *Uncontrollable shaking*
- *Chest pain*
- *Breathing is too rapid/shallow*
- *Dizzy spells*
- *Cold feet and hands*
- *Pale skin*
- *Dark circles under eyes*
- *Fatigue*

- *Feeling detached from others*
- *Not caring if you live or die*
- *Being on "auto-pilot"*
- *Headaches*
- *Loss of appetite*
- *"Nervous" eating—no satisfaction from food*
- *Pacing*
- *Nightmares (especially those in which you relive the loss)*
- *Frequent urination*

 Some of the above symptoms could also signal serious physical illness. See your doctor if you experience persistent symptoms, any kind of chest pain, or symptoms that are accompanied by fever, cough, or vomiting.

At the Heart of the Matter

If you could pick a color that describes how you feel right now about the loss in your life, which color would it be? Why? If you feel comfortable doing so, share your choice and its meaning to you with your support group.

_____

_____

_____

_____

_____

_____

_____

What scents or smells remind you of the person you lost? How does experiencing those scents impact you physically? Emotionally?

_____

_____

_____

_____

_____

_____

_____

_____

_____

To whom in your life do you turn most comfortably when you need emotional support? Explain the reasons for your answer. What qualities does this person possess that make you feel safe to confide in them?

_____

_____

_____

_____

_____

_____

_____

_____

In the space below, draw a picture that depicts the way your heart feels today. Don't be afraid to use whatever colors your mind gravitates toward.

Putting It Into Practice

Even though the physical symptoms you may be experiencing are a normal part of the grief process, you don't have to just endure them without any kind of intervention to help you feel better. Let's look at some simple ways to deal with the physical discomfort of grieving.

In the space below each symptom, jot down information concerning your own experience with it. Have you experienced the symptom? How often? Is it severe, moderate, or mild? Have you seen a doctor because of it? Are you taking any kind of medication to relieve it? (See suggested interventions.)

Sleeplessness

_____

_____

_____

(light meal at bedtime, decrease noise level, non-caffeinated herb tea)

Tense Muscles/ Tremors

_____

_____

_____

(weekly massage, calcium supplement, deep breathing exercises, daily walk)

Poor Appetite

_____

_____

_____

(small, attractive meals, eat with someone, increase fresh fruits and veggies)

Low Energy

_____

_____

_____

(early to bed and early to rise, fresh grape juice, nutritional supplements, power walk)

Chest Pain/Palpitations

_____

_____

_____

(see physician, deep breathing, no caffeine, relaxation exercises)

Headaches/Cold Hands and Feet

_____

_____

_____

(increase water intake, limit cheese, relaxation exercises, hot foot soaks)

Irritability

_____

_____

_____

(relaxation exercises, no caffeine/sugar, power walk daily, meditation/prayer)

Pale Skin/Dark Circles Under Eyes

_____

_____

_____

(increase REM sleep*, eat foods high in iron, rule out allergies, increase exercise)

Frequent Urination

_____

_____

_____

(rule out infection, increase water intake to 8-10 glasses/day, no caffeine)

Dizziness

_____

_____

_____

(rise slowly and in stages, see physician, relaxation exercises)

* REM sleep can be increased by going to bed before midnight, decreasing distractions that cause frequent sleep interruptions, and checking with your doctor for possible sleep disorders.

A Closer Look

To be able to ask for what you need at this (or any other) phase in the grief process, it is important to understand what your basic needs **are**. Have you ever stopped to think about what you really need in life? Were you raised in a home environment that met your needs and encouraged you to express your wants and desires openly without being shamed or rejected? The **emotional tone** in your family of origin can have a lot to do with how you are able to deal with your grief now.

The Open Family System

In an open family system, self-esteem of the individual family members is high. The family has few, if any, secrets. Communication is direct, clear, specific, and growth producing. It's okay to talk openly about feelings, be sad, or cry in front of other family members. It's okay to let children see adults show their emotions. It's okay to let times of crisis open up old hurts so they can be forgiven and set aside.

"Power" is equally distributed rather than one person trying to maintain control over everyone else. There are clear, consistent boundaries in this type of family. There is closeness, yet individuals are given room to be themselves. There are shared values and an ability to tolerate change and make mistakes. Spirituality is valued and nurtured.

The open family is willing to receive validation from people outside the immediate family, so it welcomes outsider's participation. Flexibility is encouraged, and family members have full freedom to comment on everything that's happening.

The Closed Family System

The rules are quite different in a closed family system. Here, there may be so many secrets you can never tell how anyone really feels. Family members who smile and say everything is okay may be hiding anger or fear that they are unable to express.

Individuals in a closed family system often have a low self-esteem. Their communication tends to be indirect, unclear, and unspecific. There may be obvious incongruities between what they are saying and what their body language is telling you. Double messages and "double binds" are common. The ability to play and be spontaneous may be absent. There is often a high tolerance for inappropriate behavior, including physical, emotional, or sexual abuse.

Maintaining the established rules is very important to closed family systems. Family members are required to change their needs to conform to the rules, which may tell them:

- **Be strong and never cry in front of each other.**

- **Never talk about anyone in the family who may be an embarrassment or somehow mar the family image.**

- **Crying and other emotional displays are a sign of weakness.**

- **Someone is always to blame.**

- **Love hurts and is supposed to be painful.**

- **Love means not having to talk.**

Closed family systems are often labeled as "dysfunctional" which simply means "living in pain".

Do you see your family of origin in one of these two descriptions? Of course, no family is completely closed or completely open. Most are a combination of the two. However, if your family is more closed than open, you may be influenced by "family rules" that encourage you to deny your real needs.

Take a look at Maslow's chart below that outlines basic human needs. When you look at the pyramid, remember that the needs at the bottom (or base) of the pyramid must be met before the higher needs can be addressed.

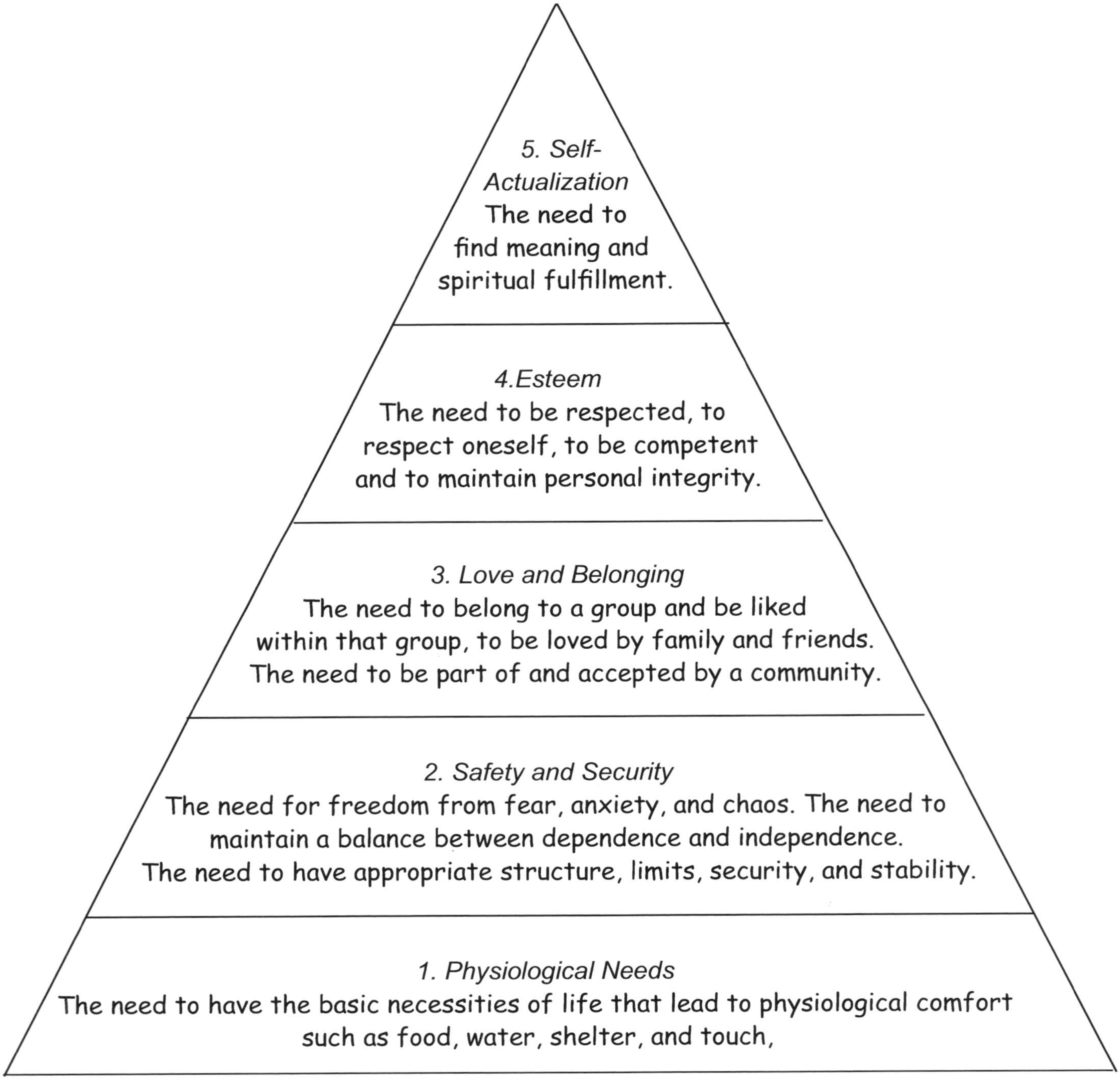

5. Self-Actualization
The need to find meaning and spiritual fulfillment.

4. Esteem
The need to be respected, to respect oneself, to be competent and to maintain personal integrity.

3. Love and Belonging
The need to belong to a group and be liked within that group, to be loved by family and friends. The need to be part of and accepted by a community.

2. Safety and Security
The need for freedom from fear, anxiety, and chaos. The need to maintain a balance between dependence and independence. The need to have appropriate structure, limits, security, and stability.

1. Physiological Needs
The need to have the basic necessities of life that lead to physiological comfort such as food, water, shelter, and touch,

Are You A Highly Sensitive Person?

In every herd of horses, cattle or deer, there are individuals that serve a special purpose to the group. They are the sensitive ones, those who first smell smoke or the scent of an enemy, and alert the rest of the group to the danger. Research has shown that all of the higher mammal species have this subgroup of sentinels, including humans. They comprise about 15% of any given population.

In centuries and millennia past, the highly sensitive humans became the spiritual leaders and the leading thinkers of the times. Highly sensitive people not only have finely attuned physical senses, such as hearing and sight and smell, they see patterns in society very readily and can make sense of these patterns in ways that others cannot. They are also often highly spiritually attuned and possess a deep level of spiritual insight.

Because of their innate perceptivity and the worldview they have developed as a result, these individuals often lend their energies and insight to causes they believe in.

What are the implications for you if you are indeed a highly sensitive? There are many, actually, and you will function much more effectively if you recognize and honor this trait as the valuable gift that it is, and shape your work and home life around it to increase your productivity and happiness on the job and everywhere else.

Characteristics of Highly Sensitive People

- Can walk into a room and sense what people are feeling in seconds

- Notice subtleties in tone, inflection and body language in others that most people would miss

- Very sensitive sense of smell and taste

- Often sensitive to perfumes, smoke and chemical odors, even if they're present in very small amounts

- Have a difficult time screening out stimuli and can feel bombarded by visual and auditory stimulation (such as a shopping trip to a department store) and feel exhausted in a short time

- Can struggle with insomnia and anxiety issues when feeling stressed

- Work better on their own time table rather than on a forced schedule since they often need time to decompress after social interactions, especially intense ones

- Need to have a high level of meaning in their work to feel that they are fulfilling their purpose in life

- Are deeply intuitive and tend to see patterns in society that others don't

- Very sensitive to others' presence in their "space," although they won't necessarily see it as an invasion depending on the situation

- Deeply wounded by careless comments or thoughtless gestures

- Tend to cry easily

- Often highly skilled at gift giving or notes of appreciation as they pick up easily on cues about what the other person would find meaningful

- Usually highly spiritually attuned, though they may not talk about it

- Move easily in different cultural settings since it comes naturally to them to notice and adapt to cultural variances

If you are a highly sensitive person, be sure you have a place to go that refreshes your heart and mind and feeds your spirit. For you, this isn't a luxury, it is a necessity.

Spend time outdoors whenever you can. Limit exposure to environments where positive ions predominate. You may want to invest in a negative ion generator.

Rest and relaxation isn't optional. You will deplete your stores of energy faster than your non-highly sensitive friends. Guard your rest as the precious treasure that it is.

Hugs

Are practically perfect:
They are low energy consumption,
High energy yield,
No monthly payments,
Non-fattening,
Inflation proof,
No pesticides,
No preservatives,
Non-taxable,
Non-polluting,
And, of course, fully returnable.

Author Unknown

3. The Many Faces of Anger
How to Make the Anger Phase of the Healing Process Work for You in Positive Ways

"Just the facts, please…"
"You shouldn't be angry."

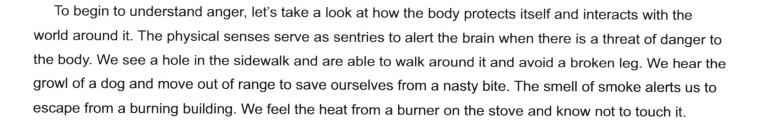

How many times have you heard those words either spoken or inferred? Many people fear anger and avoid it at all cost. But is their fear justified? Just what is the truth about anger? The anger phase of the grief process is real. It won't go away just because we don't like it. And judging ourselves harshly for having such "negative" emotions will only serve to increase our pain at a time when we have quite enough to deal with already.

To begin to understand anger, let's take a look at how the body protects itself and interacts with the world around it. The physical senses serve as sentries to alert the brain when there is a threat of danger to the body. We see a hole in the sidewalk and are able to walk around it and avoid a broken leg. We hear the growl of a dog and move out of range to save ourselves from a nasty bite. The smell of smoke alerts us to escape from a burning building. We feel the heat from a burner on the stove and know not to touch it.

The same physical senses that warn us of danger also bring us pleasure and teach us about the world we live in: the view from a mountain top, the fragrance of gardenia blossoms or an ocean mist, the sound of Beethoven's Fifth Symphony, the touch of a friend…

The emotional senses function in much the same way. They warn us of emotional danger, they convey important information about our surroundings, and they bring us the pleasure of relating to others in our world. The basic emotional senses are sadness, joy, fear, shame, and anger. Sadness alerts us that a loss has occurred that we may not be able to readily identify. It triggers a process of introspection and helps us grieve the loss. Joy lets us know that everything is going well and that our emotional and spiritual needs are being met. Fear signals a potential threat and develops into anger to alert us that our boundaries are being invaded in some way and gives us the energy we need to take some kind of corrective action. Shame helps us maintain social appropriateness and function smoothly within a group. We will discuss shame more fully in the chapter on guilt.

Some questions you may be asking...

 If anger is simply a basic emotional defense mechanism that alerts us when a boundary invasion has occurred, why is anger part of the grief process? What boundary invasion has occurred with the loss of my loved one?

To understand the ways in which a major loss is a boundary invasion, it might be helpful to review what boundaries actually are and how they function to protect us. A boundary marks the place where you end and someone else begins. When we maintain healthy boundaries, we ask to be treated with respect and we treat others with the same honor.

Boundaries don't separate and distance us from others. Quite the contrary. They make it safe for us to be close to those we care about. When we know our own boundaries, we can have healthy intimacy without becoming confused by intermingling other's needs, wants, and desires with our own. We can see clearly what belongs to us (in the emotional realm) and what belongs to them.

Individuals who have been abused as children by having their boundaries repeatedly Ignored often grow up to have either absent boundaries (and thus allow others to use and abuse them emotionally or physically) or rigid boundaries (in which case they become controlling and fixed in their determination not to let anyone "too close" for fear of being annihilated emotionally again).

Flexible boundaries are the most effective. It is very possible to express clearly and directly what we need and want while also being sensitive to how our words will affect others. We can be assertive with others without being aggressive. We can be both tender and strong, firm and respectful.

Picture yourself as an English cottage nestled in a beautiful rock garden. A white picket fence with a quaint rose trellis gate completely surrounds the cottage. Stately salvia, its purple blooms shimmering in the summer sunlight, lines the cobblestone walk. Bright pansies lift cheerful faces from their beds beside the porch.

Each room in the cottage is part of you. There is the sitting room where you keep mementos of happy times, memorabilia that you are willing to share with the guests that you invite into this part of yourself. There is the bedroom where you allow only that intimate other who shares your deepest emotions. There is another room for close friendships, one for family members that you love, and a workroom for the projects which are important to you. There may be a hidden closet that you never open because of the frightening things locked away in it: memories of deep pain, shame, guilt, or fear.

The garden surrounding your house is visible to all who pass by on the road of life. Many friends, old and new, knock at the garden gate, asking to come into your yard and sit awhile, spending time enjoying the beauty of who you are. Some you only allow into the yard or onto the porch and conversation is about the weather and the latest gardening techniques. Others you invite into your sitting room to share photos and more intimate conversation. Still others are welcomed by you into spaces reserved for the closest, most trustworthy friends.

Boundaries are represented by that picket fence that surrounds your yard, by the front door of your cottage, and by the doors on each of the rooms within your own soul. YOU have the choice of whom you will allow into your garden and into each room of your cottage. Flexible, healthy boundaries keep out undesirable elements, but let in loved ones that can be trusted to enrich and nurture your life.

A boundary invasion occurs when someone enters your "yard" or any part of your "home" without your permission. If someone jumps over your fence and starts stomping on the flowers in your garden, you have experienced a boundary invasion. A feeling of anger, characterized by a rush of blood to your face, clenched teeth and hands, pounding heart, or tight throat surges through you, thus providing you with the adrenaline necessary to deal assertively with the intruder.

Boundary invasions can occur emotionally, physically, or spiritually. Any communication that is not respectful to you is an emotional boundary invasion. Verbal put-downs, cold manipulative silences, disgusted sighs, and any kind of judging or condemning comments are all emotional abuse and are boundary invasions.

Any touch not given in love and with your permission is a physical boundary invasion. Touch withheld by an intimate other in an attempt to control or manipulate you is also physical abuse and thus is a physical boundary invasion. Any communication with you that does not totally respect your right to freedom of choice is a spiritual boundary invasion. Attempts to shame or scare you into believing in a certain way are always spiritual boundary invasions.

Major loss is a boundary invasion because it is something that happens to you without your permission that affects every room in your "house." Whether a certain individual is responsible for your loss or it is a result of circumstances beyond anyone's control, your "house" will never be the same again. So, as soon as the anesthetic of shock wears off , the "alarm system" of anger begins to sound, alerting you that something serious has happened here that requires attention.

 How will I be able to recognize the anger phase of grief? I'm not a person who throws temper tantrums or expresses anger openly. Are you sure I can't just skip this stage?

Anger has many faces. As a child, if you lived in close proximity to someone who expressed anger in a volatile, assaultive, boundary-invading way, you may grow up believing that the only way to express anger is through rage. That way of expressing anger may be so frightening and distasteful to you (justifiably so) that you learned to avoid expressing anger at all.

However, complications occur, when the anger "alarm" is ignored rather than acted upon in healthy ways. The alarm doesn't stop sounding because it is ignored. It simply finds another less healthy way to sound. It may express itself in physical ways (anger turned inward) such as migraine headaches, body aches and pains, heart problems, skin disorders, fibromyalgia, arthritis, rheumatoid arthritis, and memory problems. Or it may express itself in emotional ways such as emotional hypersensitivity, phobias, depression, panic attacks, and various addictive processes.

Signs of the Anger Phase of Grief

- Fear – of the future, of the dark, of going on with life, of not being able to go on with life, of being alone…

- Reliving the loss over and over and over again, trying to make sense of it

- Feeling isolated and estranged from loved ones because you don't want them to know how angry you are that the loss happened

- Physical manifestations such as sleeplessness, tension headaches, muscle tightness, chest pain, etc.

- Feeling irritable with those who are moving on with their lives as if the loss didn't make any difference to them

- Feeling that you want to "run away" from your life as it is now

- Difficulty concentrating on tasks—your mind always goes back to the loss and the implications for your life

- Seeing others with their loved ones and feeling angry that you don't have your loved one now

Purposes of the Anger Phase of Grief

- To provide energy and motivation to deal with the added responsibilities created by the loss

- To mobilize the brain to deal with the tasks of grieving

- To provide an opportunity for processing old, unresolved issues

- To create enough emotional momentum to push past any walls of denial that may prevent emotional honesty with yourself and others

At the Heart of the Matter

Someone once said, "When you feel angry, look for the hidden fear, for it is always there." It is for this reason that anger is often considered a secondary emotion. Identifying the threat (loss) is the first step towards dealing with the fear and the anger that it triggers.

What fears have you experienced as a result of your loss? In what ways has the loss triggered old fears from previous losses? Write your answers in the space below. If you feel comfortable doing so, share your insights with the group.

_____

_____

_____

_____

_____

_____

_____

_____

_____

_____

_____

_____

_____

_____

_____

What if.....

How many losses have you experienced over the course of your life? People often don't recognize that any change we experience in our lives is a loss. Have you had the opportunity to grieve each loss and heal? The following tool is a personal loss index. In the spaces provided, jot down the events as they occurred in your life. Be as comprehensive as possible.

My Personal Index of Losses

Births (My own experience—difficult? Separated from mom? Premie? Other births—of my siblings, my own children, abortions, etc.)

Relationship changes involving children and parents (Child to boarding school? Parent's divorce? Parent working out of town and gone a lot?)

Changes in schools or teachers

Changes in place of residence

Illnesses or Injuries—short or long term

Surgeries or other serious medical procedures

Holidays, family reunions, birthdays, anniversaries
(Letting go of the "old" and moving into the "new" with each one)

Marriages/Divorces

Employment history (Jobs lost or gained-major change each time, being fired)

Any incidences of assault or abuse (to youself or witnessing it happening to someone else - 9/11, mass shootings, etc.)

Significant relationships (Beginning, ongoing, ending)

Aging process

Periods of success (Often more stressful than failure!)

Financial losses or gains

Natural disasters experienced (Fire, earthquake, hurricane, tornado, flood)

Retirement

Deaths

When you have completed your loss index, if reading this as part of a group, divide into teams of two or three and discuss which losses stand out in your mind as being unresolved and ungrieved (possibly because you didn't recognize them as losses).

In the space below, write a letter to your inner child about the losses you have sustained and how they relate to the major loss you are now experiencing.

Putting It Into Practice

If you haven't started one already, now is an excellent time to begin a daily journal to process the feelings that ebb and flow as you progress through your journey to healing. The kind of notebook you use is not nearly as important as making a decision to consistently write in it. This is a time in your life when consistency may take some extra effort, but when it comes to journaling, the reward is well worth it.

Here are some hints that may help make your journaling experience more effective and meaningful:

Make a decision to be committed to the process.

Growth and healing are painful. There is no way around it. Facing our feelings can sometimes create waves of pain that may seem overwhelming at times, especially if we have avoided facing them in the past.

You may feel that if you start crying you'll never stop, so you avoid facing those thoughts and feelings that bring you to tears. You may feel afraid that you will alienate loved ones by admitting the deep anger you feel. The truth is that you will stop crying eventually, no matter how much pain you release on paper. And the chances are good that you won't alienate loved ones by being honest with them and letting them know just where you are in your grief process, instead they will feel closer to you because you are being real with them.

Choose a regular time and a special place for journaling.

It takes about 30 days of continuing in a certain behavior pattern to create new brain pathways that are deep enough to regulate our behavior. Until then, it will take effort to remember to journal. "Tagging" your journaling time to some other activity will help you remember to do it during those days and weeks before it becomes a routine. You may want to journal every morning right after you brush your teeth. Or at night as soon as you put the cat out. Or every day during your lunch break.

Remember the purpose.

Therapeutic journaling is not a "left-brained" activity. Its purpose is *not* to chronicle factual events like "I bought a new pair of pants today" or "Three people came to my stamping party last night."

Its purpose *is* to process emotions. How did you feel about buying the new pair of pants and coming home to an empty house with no one to notice them or comment on how they look on you? Were the three people who came to your party supportive or was there an awkward silence that reminded you of how uncomfortable many people are in the presence of grief?

Processing means *releasing*. The opposite of processing is repression (denial and dishonesty). It's amazing how much we hide from ourselves when the truth seems too painful to face. As we honestly, openly, and courageously examine our thoughts and feelings, we circumvent the possibility that our normal grief-anger could harden into bitterness or that the fear that is triggered by deep loss could create a wall of self-protectiveness, cutting us off from our own true selves.

A Closer Look

When do you think that fear ceases its positive function as an alarm system and becomes destructive? What about anger?

_____

_____

_____

_____

_____

_____

"Faith is fear turned inside out."
Author Unknown

"You gain strength, courage, and confidence by every experience
in which you really stop to look fear in the face.
You must do the thing which you think you cannot do.

Eleanor Roosevelt

"Without darkness,
nothing comes to birth
As without light,
nothing flowers."
May Sarton

Victim mentality is a condition that can seriously cripple a person in the anger phase of the grief process. This mind-set develops in the face of long-term unresolved grief, usually beginning in early childhood. A child who is abused physically, emotionally, and spiritually has experienced tremendous loss and often grows up into an adult who is "stuck" in all three areas. Trust in others is broken and true connection with a support system is very difficult.

The emotional and spiritual pain that accompanies victim mentality can profoundly affect the person's ability to move through the tasks of grieving. The person is often unable to see the options available for healing. Full-blown fear, bitterness, despair, depression, loneliness, hopelessness, confusion, rage, apathy, shame, hatred, helplessness, and a spirit of revenge are common symptoms of this condition.

If you sense that you may be stuck in this painful victim role, there are principles you can apply to begin the healing process and help you find the strength you need to face your fears. It will be highly beneficial to you to share honestly with your group and will also be helpful to you to find a personal counselor to work with you in more specific ways on the early childhood issues that brought you to this place in your adult life.

<u>Acceptance</u>

Acceptance is the opposite of control. Trying to control others is futile, but if you find yourself stuck in victim mentality, you will probably attempt it anyway because you feel helpless and afraid. You may try desperately to maintain control over people and circumstances in your life to allay the fear. This fear can be greatly magnified during the anger phase of grief.

Healthy acceptance acknowledges that the only person I can control is myself. It respects the boundaries of others and lets go of any attempt to change or coerce them in any way. It may help to repeat a prayer from the 12 Step program of Alcoholics Anonymous:

> **God grant me the serenity to accept**
> **the things I cannot change,**
> **the courage to change the things I can,**
> **and the wisdom to know the difference.**

To Let Go...

Does not mean to stop caring,
It means you can't do it for someone else.
Is not to cut myself off,
It's the realization that I can't control another.

Is not to enable,
But to allow learning from natural consequences.
Is to admit I am powerless,
Which simply means the outcome is not in my hands.

Is not to try to change another,
It's to make the most of myself.
Is not to care for,
but to care about .

Is not to fix,
But to be supportive.
Is not to judge,
But to allow another to be a human being.

Is not to be in the middle arranging all the outcomes,
But to allow others to affect their own destinies.
Is not to be protective,
It's to permit another to face reality.

Is not to criticize or regulate anyone,
But to become all that I can be.

To LET GO is to FEAR LESS

Author Unknown

49

Encouragement

One of the great principles of the universe in which we live is the Law of Attraction. Very simply put, we reap what we sow. In very real and measurable ways, the thoughts that we nurture eventually become our reality.

A characteristic of victim mentality is a martyr complex. Instead of finding positive things to appreciate in others, these hurting people can only focus on their own pain. They tend to be highly critical of others, but only because they are even more critical of themselves, calling themselves "realistic" in their outlook on life.

Encouragement can be applied to a bruised spirit much as a healing salve to a physical wound, although the hurting person must make the choice to receive the support. The best news of all is that the wounded person doesn't have to wait for someone else to come along and apply this remedy.

Making the choice to speak only respectful and encouraging words about yourself and others is a crucial component of emotional and spiritual healing. Your mind cannot differentiate between shaming, critical words spoken **by you** to or about others, spoken **to you** by others, or spoken **to you by yourself**. They are all registered as a wound in your own heart and they all damage you.

And, with equal power, words spoken to you or by you that are respectful and supportive will uplift and strengthen you and result in improved emotional and spiritual health. Think about it. What do you say when you make a mistake of some kind? Do you shame and berate yourself? Or do you say, "That's okay, I learned something from that. It was a good attempt."

Learning to engage in positive self-talk is one of the greatest challenges of the person with a victim mentality, but it is possible to change old wounding habits and make a solid choice to speak only words of encouragement and support.

Forgiveness

Without forgiveness there can be no healing. Harboring un-forgiveness toward someone has been likened to taking arsenic and waiting for the other person to die. Forgiveness does not involve a case of amnesia in which you are able to mentally erase the wrongs of others and never bring them to mind again. It is **not** a passive acceptance of anything anyone else chooses to do to you. And it does not happen instantly.

It **is** a process that begins with a decision to forgive and follows the grief process through from denial to acceptance, where forgiveness is completed. Forgiveness is a courageous act of the will. It is a decision to accept the pain of the grief process and let go of the need for revenge. It is a choice to have compassion on the person who hurt you. (Although you may not choose to be in active relationship with that person, if they are still living, if they are not safe to be in relationship with.)

Those suffering with victim mentality are most often stuck at the point of forgiveness. Their pain is so deep it seems impossible to forgive those who have wounded them so seriously. If you feel you are stuck here, express your feelings to the group and enlist their support in moving forward. Other groups that can support you in your journey are twelve step groups such as Adult Children of Alcoholics (ACOA), Al-Anon, or Codependents Anonymous.

Archbishop Desmond Tutu, as chairman of South Africa's Truth and Reconciliation Commission from 1995-1997, listened as 21,000 witnesses described to him the atrocities committed in South Africa during the apartheid era. He wept openly as he heard the terrible stories. His response when all was revealed? Forgiveness.

"With forgiveness we open the door for someone who might have been shackled to the past to break loose the shackles and walk into a new future."

More likely than not, the person who will be freed by the forgiveness you choose to extend to those who have wittingly or unwittingly hurt you, will be you.

Gratitude

This remedy is one of the hardest to apply when the suffocating weight of grief threatens to snuff out every joy from life. How can one be thankful when the pain is so great? Here again it takes a choice, an act of the will, to change the internal atmosphere of the heart.

Called in 12 Step circles the "attitude of gratitude", this amazingly effective exercise is so simple it is hard to believe it could make such a difference. To apply it, take the time each day to list the things in your life that you are grateful for. Simple things. Everyday, common things that make the difference in your quality of life. Start with twenty-five things. Increase it to thirty. Then fifty. The grass under your feet. The seagulls wheeling over the bay. The dandelions in the yard. The color purple. Your daughter's smile...

Try it. You'll be amazed by the spiritual energy it generates. Guaranteed.

Meditation and Prayer

Whatever your spiritual background or your concept of God, meditation and prayer can help you. These activities have been scientifically proven through double-blind studies to improve physical health as well as provide emotional and spiritual strength. People who pray and spend time in quiet meditation experience more rapid healing of body and mind after a trauma. Meditation also lowers the blood pressure and improves cardiac function.

Find a quiet, comfortable place to meditate where you will not be disturbed by a phone ringing or people moving about and interrupting your time alone. Take slow deep breaths in through your nose and out through your mouth, becoming aware of each different part of your body and what that part is feeling. It often helps to visualize a peaceful place that generates a feeling of serenity and safety in your heart. It could be a mountain cabin next to a rushing stream with a wildflower-dotted meadow stretching up to the snowline or the warm sand of a tropical beach with swaying palms and waves rolling in to the shore.

This time of quiet will allow you to connect with the spiritual part of you that hungers for peace and quiet renewal. Whatever form your religious practice takes, it will be enhanced by being in touch with your own heart in this way.

Ojibwa Prayer

Oh Great Spirit,
Whose voice I hear in the winds
And whose breath
Gives life to everyone,
Hear me.

I come to you as one of your many children;
I am weak
I am small
I need your wisdom and your strength.
Let me walk in beauty, and make my eyes ever
behold the red and purple sunsets.

Make my hands respect the things you have made,
and make my ears sharp so
I may hear your voice.
Make me wise, so that
I may understand what you
have taught my people and
The lessons you have hidden in each leaf
and each rock.
I ask for wisdom and strength,
Not to be superior to my
brothers, but to be able
to fight my greatest enemy, myself.
Make me ever ready to come before you with
clean hands and a straight eye,
So as life fades away as a fading sunset,
My spirit may come to you without shame.

Author Unknown

4. Making a Deal With God
How to Find Personal Growth and Greater Healing in the Bargaining Phase of Grief

"Just the facts, please...

In an old Twilight Zone episode, a thug finds out that his soldier son is dying of a bullet wound in a faraway country. In an attempt at prayer, the first in his life, he begs God to spare his son and to take him instead. His prayer is answered and the son lives, unaware of the sacrifice his father made for him.

A young woman promises herself to quit smoking when her mother is diagnosed with lung cancer. Her children suddenly become very obedient and compliant in their actions when they learn that "Grandma is sick". The grandmother, who is facing a terminal illness, starts going back to the synagogue of her childhood for the first time in years.

Two years pass and the chemotherapy treatments have been unsuccessful. In spite of the physicians' best efforts, the woman dies of lung cancer. After the shock has given way to anger, the daughter begins to realize how vulnerable she really is, too. She thinks of how short and how fragile life is. She becomes very concerned about her own children's safety and monitors their every move. She lectures them on the dangers of smoking and urges them to promise her that they will never take up the habit . Somehow, it sees that if she can just convince her children not to follow in her mother's footsteps, all the pain of losing her mother will have had some kind of meaning.

Once the anger phase of grief has subsided, it is common for a grieving person to move into some form of bargaining. It may not be as obvious as the cases presented here. Bargaining can be totally non-verbal and the bargainer may not be aware of his behavior at all. Making a choice to stop a bad habit, becoming "nicer" to family and friends, making amends for old hurts, increasing donations to charities, throwing oneself into meaningful community activities… These can all be a form of bargaining if done in an effort to regain "control" over one's life and somehow help relieve the pain of the loss.

Some questions you may be asking...

 What are some of the signs of the bargaining phase of grief?

• **Increased attention paid to the tenets of one's belief system** (Making vows to attend church, synagogue, or mosque with renewed dedication. Increased prayer, often characterized by asking for a certain outcome)

• **A personal change for the "better" in the way the person deals with others** (More compliant, more understanding, more forgiving, or easier to get along with than is the "norm" for them)

• **Major change in one or more lifestyle habits** (May give up drinking, smoking, overeating, etc).

• **Changes in financial priorities** (May choose to give more money to the charity of their choice)

• **Taking up a cause that benefits others in similar situations to the loved one that was lost** (Mothers Against Drunk Drivers is an organization formed by a mom whose child was killed by a drunk driver)

If the person in the bargaining phase of grief is not fully aware that they are bargaining in an attempt to regain some of the control they have lost, how can this experience help them grow and heal?

Human growth and development can be a rather complex process, and each person embarks on his own growth journey at his own speed and in his own way. Even if we are not aware of the healing that is happening within us as we progress through the grief process, it is still going on. We don't have to be cognizant of the fact that we are bargaining for control to benefit from the in-depth spiritual inventory that results from all of our questions and crying out for answers.

Fortunately or unfortunately, however we choose to view it, we as humans tend to be much more teachable when we are flattened by grief and straining for answers and explanations and ways to do something about our pain. It is during this stage of the grief process that many people deal with unresolved spiritual issues from their past. What begins as tragedy in our lives often, due to the soul searching that results, generates some of the greatest personal growth we will ever experience.

At the Heart of the Matter

Take a few moments to pause and reflect on your loss. Then close your eyes and picture yourself sitting on a grassy knoll overlooking the ocean or on a bench beside a bamboo fountain in a peaceful Japanese garden with a spiritual figure who is important in your life sitting beside you. Imagine the conversation you would have with him or her about the loss you've experienced in your life. What would you ask? What would you say about how you are feeling right now? What would you ask about the future? Write your thoughts in the space below. Then, if you are working with a group, share your feelings if you are comfortable doing so.

Draw a picture in the space below that depicts "hope" to you.

Putting It Into Practice

During this next week, stay alert to your own reactions to others, to yourself, and to God. Address these reactions each day in your journal. Do you find yourself feeling helpless? Angry? Overwhelmed? Peeved? Appreciated? Timid? Fearful? Relieved?

Grief magnifies our reactions, but it doesn't cause them. This is an ideal time to do some processing of our deepest responses to life. These responses have their roots in our earliest experiences in life, when our emotions were forming.

Looking back to childhood experiences is not healing in and of itself, but identifying early "misprogramming" in our emotions can clue us in to what core beliefs about life we may need to let go of to allow our selves to be "reprogrammed" in healthy, healing ways.

Was your home environment shaming and critical? If so, you may have many harsh "tapes" set up in your mind, ready to be triggered into playing by the least hint of criticism from an outside source. Often, the trigger doesn't even have to come from an outside person. You can start those tapes easily all by yourself in reaction to anything in your day that you perceive as pointing up your inadequacies. (I should have done a better job on that… I didn't get as much done today as I should have .. I should be a kinder person… I didn't even say thank you when that woman held the door open for me… I shouldn't yell at the kids, even though they spilled grape juice on the new carpet. Etc., etc.)

> ⟨!⟩ *Major Hint:* **Anytime you hear yourself say the word** *should*, **be alert for some kind of old tape being triggered.** *Should* **is a shaming word and causes damage when it is used, whether you are saying it to yourself or to someone else Replace the word** *should* **with the phrase** *I choose to…* **or** *I will….*

Was your childhood home environment neglectful or abusive, emotionally or physically? If so, you are likely to have trigger points of fear and pain inside you that are left over from those early years. This current loss may well trigger those fears and the pain of having someone abandon you who was "supposed to" love you and stay close to you always.

As you process your reactions this week by writing about them in your journal, try to identify the early triggers that are causing the reaction. Ask yourself, "When did I very first feel this way?" It may seem difficult at first, but you will be surprised how many memories surface in the face of a triggering event.

Five Keys to Identifying a Reaction

• **Emotion wells up inside that is much stronger than the stimulus deserves.**

• **A feeling of helplessness kicks in, similar to the way a young child feels when he or she doesn't know how to handle the situation at hand.**

• **Body language and voice tone may take on the characteristics of a young child. (I.e.: "He's acting like a two year old.")**

• **Coping skills tend to fly out the window as regression occurs.**

• **Fear takes over.**

A Closer Look

As time goes on and your journaling continues, you will be able to recognize yourself in reaction much more quickly than ever before. Take a look at the following list and see if your reactions fit under any of these headings:

Self Pity

"I can't do it"
"I'm no good"
"I may as well give up"
"I'm stupid"
(jealousy, envy, despair, fear)

Entitlement

"They're stupid"
"If only they hadn't interfered,
I'd have been able to"
"That idiot"
"It's all her fault"
(pride, greed, lust, rage)

Self-righteousness

"I can do it myself"
"I'm as good as he is"
"I'm not as bad as you think I am"
(Perfectionism, judgment, apathy, prejudice)

Relationship is the Only Thing That Can Heal Reaction!

Move into relationship as soon as you sense a reaction in yourself. Pick up that thousand pound phone and call your accountability or support partner. Talk to a friend. Talk to God. Open your heart to someone, even if it just means saying, "Help!".

Allow others to pour empathy and acceptance on you. This is where the healing starts. We don't need help with our positive emotions. It's the "negative" ones that create a sense of shame and isolation. The shame response has often been programmed into us at a very early age. It's time to create new neural pathways by responding to our own emotions with compassion and understanding instead of guilt and shame.

Be alert for new insights about your reaction. The healing process continues as you allow yourself to be accepted, supported, and lovingly challenged by your safe group. Listen to what they might have to say to you about what they've observed.

Take positive action. This will cement the healing lessons you are learning in your mind, moving them out of the realm of theory and into the world of experience. This is where most of the actual healing happens.

**We do not see things as they are.
We see things as we are.**

The Talmud

5. In the Valley of the Shadow
*How to Gain Strength and Perspective
from the Depression Stage of Grief*

"Just the facts, please..."

Someone once said, "Grief is the noblest emotion." If this is true, it is in the depression stage of grief that the nobility is developed. Once the anesthetic of denial has worn off, the anger phase of grief has done its motivating work, and the time for bargaining has passed, taking with it any hope for a reversal of the painful circumstances, the real work of grief begins.

For that is just what grief is: hard work. This stage could best be described as a time of deep sadness and reflection. It is a time in which the full impact of the loss hits home. It is a time of deep, creative pain.

The Western culture emphasizes pain control. If your head hurts, hurry to the store to buy a bottle of aspirin. If you have emotional pain, distract yourself from it immediately with alcohol or prescription drugs. In the grief process, pain is unavoidable and must be experienced for healing to happen. The sooner we embrace and feel the sadness and learn its creative lesson, the sooner we will heal.

Grief is not an illness. The sadness stage of grief is not something abnormal to be fixed. It is where we give the relationship we have lost its deepest honor. It is a soul salute to someone irreplaceable.

It is also an opportunity. Our lives are often a frantic whirl of activity. Where is the center of quietness that is so necessary for the development of wisdom and perspective? Grief, especially in the depression stage, stops us in our tracks and offers us the opportunity to discover more deeply who we are.

Some questions you may be asking...

 ## How can I tell I am in the depression stage of grief?

This stage in the grief process is characterized by a sense of deep and profound sadness. The full impact of the loss is hitting, without the numbing benefit of denial or the distractions of anger and bargaining. Here are some reflections on how it feels to be in the depression stage of grief from those who have experienced it:

"It felt as if I were falling into a dark chasm with no bottom. I couldn't see any end to the pain."

"For a long time, I felt so angry that he had just up and left me. How could he turn his back on all that we had together? I focused on the bad things that had happened in our relationship to try to convince myself that I am better off without him. Then the deep sadness hit and I could remember it all, good and bad, and a deep, keening sense of loss took over. I thought it was going to smother me."

"I couldn't even get out of bed in the morning. Every small task of everyday life felt impossible to me. How could I go on with my life when the best part of me, the part I gave to her, is gone?"

"It surprised me each day when the sun came up and everyone just went on with their lives as if everything was the same as ever. I wanted to scream at them that nothing is the same and deep inside me I know that it never will be again."

At the Heart of the Matter

In the depression stage of grief, because your heart is fully aware of its pain and loss, you may notice that you are "triggered" a lot. A familiar place, a certain scent, the way the air feels, a particular sound associated with your loved one, all can send you tumbling into the abyss of active grief.

It is tempting when this happens to do anything possible to relieve the pain and try to feel better again. As natural as this urge to anesthetize the pain is, growth and healing happens when you allow yourself to fully experience the loss.

The key is to not do it alone. Imagine yourself, as you think of being triggered and feeling the free fall into pain beginning, being held in the palm of God's hand or being held up by the loved ones in your support system. Allow your emotions to come in whatever form they take without trying to edit or minimize them. In the space below, draw a picture of your grief being held by God or by loved ones.

In the space below, write a letter to your grief. Describe how you perceive it. How does it feel to you? What forms does it take? Is it warm or cold? Is it smooth or prickly or slimy? What color is it? What does it taste like? What does it smell like? How does it impact your quiet time? Your work life? Your sleep? Your appetite? Your relationships? Your self-concept?

Now, in the space below, write a letter from your grief back to you.* In it, allow your grief to express to you what it is doing for you, what it is helping you to remember, what it is teaching you, and in what ways you are growing that would never have been possible had you not suffered as you have with this loss.

*(This is a technique adapted from the one first taught by Bob Deits, Growing Through Loss Workshop Conference)

Putting It Into Practice

To be able to tackle the hard work of grief, it is important to know what grief work actually looks like. What is meant by "working through your grief"? The following formula, used extensively in all areas of emotional healing, including grief work, is this:

 **Applied Information**

+

 **Loving Support**

+

 **Time**

=

 **Healing**

From the beginning of this grief manual you have been working out this healing formula. As we examined the ways that loss is a wound, what to expect at different time intervals, and what denial, anger, and bargaining look like in the grief process, you were gleaning **information** about your grieving. Each time you write out the answers to questions concerning your own reactions and feelings, you are **applying** that information to your own experience and getting in touch with more of your own truth about your loss.

As you share your innermost thoughts, feelings, and responses with the group you are working with or trusted friends, you are receiving **loving support**. It is an act of **grace** on the part of your group and friends when we share our deepest emotions, even the ones that society often looks upon as negative, and we are received, accepted, and loved. Without this **loving acceptance** by safe others, we will remain isolated and lonely, unable to feel understood and heard.

Finally, healing takes **time**. Part of the difficulty of grief work is the length of time it takes to begin to feel whole again. It is tempting as weeks turn to months, and months to years, to give up on the healing process. It feels at times as if no progress is being made. Your personal journal, in which you record your deepest feelings and thoughts, is an invaluable tool for charting your progress and encouraging yourself when you feel that the healing process is too slow. Just go back through what you have written so far and read what you wrote. You'll be surprised at what you learn about your own personal growth.

Here are some guidelines for doing "grief work" that you may find helpful:

• **Make a contract with yourself.**

Pledge to fully experience the grief process and not shy away from it. Write the contract on a note card, or a piece of quality paper, sign and date it, and hang it up someplace where you can see it many times a day. Remember that your grief is in memorial to someone very special and your grief work honors their memory.

- **Develop a support community.**

     It is not possible to do grief work alone. Isolation keeps the grief buried deep inside and prevents it from surfacing where it can be worked through. If you are comfortable doing so, exchange phone numbers with other members if you are working with a group and keep in touch with each other during the week between meetings. Eating together is especially healing, since mealtimes are a social time and can be very lonely without someone to share them with.

- **Ask for help when you need it.**

     It is a good idea to develop a 911 list of people that you can call on for different needs as they arise. This list could include people who could provide for physical needs such as someone to do yard work, wash the windows, or walk the dog. Emotional needs, however, are just as important. Which friend likes to visit antique stores and would be a great shopping buddy on an overcast, gloomy Monday when your spirits need a lift and your heart needs company?

- **Don't try to hurry the healing process.**

     You can't speed it up. Grief has its own timetable and, although you can slow it down by refusing to do the grief work, you can't force it to go faster. Learn to accept its rhythm and trust that it is moving forward even when it doesn't feel like it.

- **Be honest with yourself about where the loss really is.**

     One woman who lost her mother to cancer wasn't especially close to her. Her mother had been emotionally distant and abusive during the woman's childhood and the relationship had never healed. The woman was surprised when she experienced deep and profound grief at her mother's funeral and in the months that followed. As she looked honestly at what she had lost, she realized that she wasn't grieving her mother's death as much as she was grieving the loss of a dream, the dream that someday her mother would apologize for her abuse and want to be in relationship with her. If the woman had refused to "think ill of the dead" and had avoided looking at the real issues with her mother, she would have shut down her grief process with denial.

Avoid self-criticism.

It's easy to get down on ourselves when we feel we aren't functioning "up to par". Just keep in mind that "par" for the grief process is vastly different than it is when we are healed and whole. It may be "par" for you to spend the whole day crying when some sound or smell that reminds you of your loved one triggers deep sadness in your heart. Don't let anyone (including yourself!) tell you that you must "pull yourself together and get on with life". You will get on with life as you are ready to. Tears are healing. Allow them to flow. And when you are ready to move on, allow yourself to do that, too.

Sticks in a bundle are unbreakable.

Kenyan Proverb

Accept the seasons of your heart, even as you have always accepted the seasons that pass over your fields.

Kahlil Gibran

A Closer Look

Losing a loved one is a heavy burden to bear whatever the circumstances. There are some situations that can make the grief even more difficult to deal with. Let's take a look at some of the factors that can complicate grief and hamper healing:

- ## When there are deep, unresolved issues with the person who died

 The depth and intensity of grief with any loss is directly proportionate to the impact the person has had on our lives. When there is a strong emotional connection with someone, losing them pulls at the very roots of our soul. When the relationship was positive and there are many happy memories, it feels more natural to engage in rituals that honor the person's memory and, even in the sadness, celebrate the connection we had (and always will have in our heart) with them.

When unresolved emotional issues are present, there is confusion and difficulty engaging in the necessary rituals of grieving . The person may have had a negative impact on our life but it creates an intense connection nonetheless. It will probably require the assistance of a good counselor to work through the complex issues of this kind of grief.

- ## When the death was a suicide

Anger, guilt, intense searching and pining, and ripping pain are common bedfellows when the death was a suicide. Anger can be directed at the medical profession (for not doing something to prevent the suicide), at the one who died (for abandoning and rejecting you by choosing death rather than stay with you), at God (for not intervening), at yourself (for not being able to stop the suicide), or just at the very fact that it happened at all.

Guilt is present in some form or another with all losses (to be discussed in Chapter 6) but in the case of suicide, it can be overwhelming. "If only I had listened more..." "If only I had known how much pain she was in..." "If only I had said _____ ..." "If only I'd gotten home a little earlier..."

Those who have lost loved ones to suicide often search for the loved one for months, even years, after the death. Lois Bloom, in her little booklet "Mourning After Suicide" (The Pilgrim Press, Cleveland, Ohio) talks of searching the streets on her way home from work looking for her son who had committed suicide months earlier. She knew "in her head" it was irrational, but her heart kept searching and hoping to see him again.

A good support system is especially important if you are grieving the loss of a loved one through suicide. Many cities have support groups just for processing this kind of grief. The presence of friends and family is also crucial to your healing. Make a decision to reach out and connect with those who are able to provide you with loving support.

- **When the person who died was a child**

There is something about the death of a child that rips at our hearts in a way that nothing else can. It doesn't seem right. If feels unfair. It feels as if the future has been snatched away so very prematurely from an innocent victim. We are somewhat prepared to lose our parents as they age and have lived a full and meaningful life. But a child? How can it be time to let them go?

Losing a child can create an intense amount of guilt in the surviving parents. Where did I go wrong? How could I have prevented this from happening? Often, the intense anger and guilt that accompanies the death of a child can cause severe communication problems in the parents' relationship. Private family therapy, in addition to group support, is crucial during this time when life seems to be unraveling at the seams.

- ## When the person's body cannot be recovered

Closure is an important part of the healing process. For millennia, humans have been laying out their dead to be viewed and touched to help the living accept the finality of the loved one's death. When the body has been lost at sea or on Mt. Everest or in a fire and cannot be recovered, closure becomes very difficult. There is a lingering feeling that the person isn't really dead and they will show up some day. This lack of closure produces an enormous amount of stress in the griever's body. Emotional energy needed for the healing process is siphoned away into searching and pining.

If you have a loved one whose body has not been recovered, you may find it helpful to create a closure ritual just for you in which you tell your heart that the person is really gone and give your emotions a chance to say a final goodbye. The memorial service is helpful, but you will probably need something more personal just for you, such as burying a symbolic item. Take someone with you who understands your need for closure and can support you emotionally as you say your own personal good bye.

- ## When no rituals are performed

More and more, families in the Western part of the world and in some parts of Europe are opting not to have a funeral or a memorial service when a loved one dies. "We have to get on with our lives. The service won't bring them back," they say. Experts in the area of grief and bereavement are alarmed by this trend, which reflects the disconnection and isolation of Western society today.

The rituals performed at a memorial service are not for the person who died, they are for us. We need a chance to say goodbye to move on with our healing process. We can't reinvest in life if we don't acknowledge and grieve our losses.

Rituals such as funerals, wakes, candle lighting vigils, memorial services, flowers at the graveside, and shrines to the lost loved one are necessary exercises of the heart that connect us to our own emotions about the loss as well as honor the person who died. They give us inner "hooks" to hang our grief on.

If your family is one who opted for no rituals when your loved one died, it is not too late for you to create your own rituals. If your family won't join you, find a trusted friend or two to help you take the necessary steps to creating a ritual that will be meaningful and healing for your heart.

- **When the person died violently**

Intense anger is often the most predominate emotion when someone takes the life of our loved one through a violent act. The anger can be all consuming because the loss is based on the choices of another human being to dehumanize our loved one to the point of taking their life away. Everything in us screams for justice. It is normal to have feelings of wanting to see the person punished so that some kind of balance can be restored.

Any act of intimidation from one person to another is dehumanizing. The bully, in his own fear and insecurity, finds a victim upon whom to vent his rage toward his own weakness. He destroys an innocent life because of his own issues and everything in us shouts, "Foul play! You didn't even know him! How could you take the life of my loved one so callously and snuff it out as if he were an ant on the ground?"

When a loved one is murdered, the intense grief rises, not only in response to the immediate loss, but also in response to every act of dehumanization that has happened to us or around us since our earliest childhood experiences. Grief is cumulative and unless you have had a chance to work through childhood abuse issues (parents, teachers, bullies on the playground, etc.), your responses to this deep loss will be compounded many times over. This is an opportunity to uncover many hidden wounds. Find a good counselor and ask them to do a timeline of your childhood experiences with you. You may be amazed at what you discover.

Even the worst in life
may reveal the best of life
if one works to make it so.

Edgar N. Jackson

6. The Ravages of Remorse

Dealing with Guilt Feelings And the Crippling Effect They Can Have on the Healing Process

"Just the facts, please..."

"It's my fault. I should have been paying closer attention. This never would have happened had I been a better parent."

These are the words of a mother in the throes of guilt following a fatal accident involving one of her children. The emotional roller coaster that accompanies such a tragedy is devastating enough without the wrenching pain of guilt. When the self-condemnation beings, the load is crushing.

When a tragedy occurs involving one of our loved ones, whether it is an expected death from cancer or some other disease, or a sudden and unexpected death by accident or attack, it is common for guilt to arise. If we can just blame someone, it feels as if we have some kind of control over the situation. As the feelings of helplessness and hopelessness well up inside, assigning guilt gives us the illusion that we are taking action

This illusion, however, is not helpful in our healing process. Blame, whether directed toward others or ourselves, is a particularly harmful form of self-deception and takes us all the way back to the denial stage of grief.

The reality is that we cannot prevent bad things from happening. The truth is that we are fallible, weak, and often helpless human beings. We may not always understand why things happen the way they do. Guilt keeps us paralyzed and focused on the illusion instead of on the truth.

What does guilt look like in the grief process? How can I tell if it is unhealthy guilt?

First of all, let's look at unhealthy guilt. The following are some of the ways that guilt can paralyze us and prevent healing from taking place:

Survivor Guilt

This kind of guilt says that it isn't fair that you are still alive when your loved one isn't. It also kicks in as you grow and change past where your loved one had grown before his or her death. It tells you that to move on and do something new or different with your life is disloyal to the one no longer with you.

Depression

This is not the clinical depression that is caused by a chemical imbalance in the brain nor is it the deep, reality-based sadness that is one of the stages of the grief process. The depression that is instigated by guilt is a downward spiral that feeds on itself. It is fueled by the belief that if only you were a "better person" or had done the "right thing", this terrible loss would not have happened.

Magical Thinking

Magical thinking is a carry-over from childhood when we believed that just by imagining something in our minds we could make it happen. Often, when a parent dies, a child will believe that the death was a result of bad feelings the child carried toward the parent. When the guilt feelings hit, it's okay to recognize them as residual emotions from childhood and let them go.

Blaming

Blaming is a defense mechanism that keeps us stuck by focusing our attention on a "symbol" of our anger. Guilt feelings are incredibly painful and blaming prevents us from seeing reality, thus numbing our pain somewhat. The price tag for this anesthetic, however, is enormous. Healing can only come as we move through the grief process, facing our feelings and accepting the truth about the loss as we are ready. Blaming blocks the truth from our conscious minds and keeps us stuck in frozen grief that can last a lifetime if the blaming patterns continue. The toll on our physical, emotional, and spiritual health is tremendous.

Victim Mentality

Victim mentality is learned helplessness. Healthy humans are a balance of weakness and strength. Our *weakness* tells us that we need each other's help and support and our *strength* tells us that we are capable of great acts of faith, courage, and love-inspired creativity.

Physical, sexual, or verbal abuse (criticism included) in childhood can throw us out of balance, teaching us to access only our weakness. Because "strength" feels so unfamiliar, we avoid it and choose to stay stuck in helplessness.

Guilt and shame are the hallmarks of victim mentality, reinforcing the illusion of weakness and preventing forward momentum. If you are stuck here, go back and reread the Putting it Into Practice section in Chapter Four.

Conviction (as in "convinced of a better way") always invites us to a healthier and more complete place. If we have truly hurt someone by our actions, we will identify the error and take action to make amends.

Letting go of the unhealthy guilt does not mean that we won't feel the weight of grief or experience the anger or sadness of the grief process. It does mean that we are not carrying the world on our shoulders, responsible for everything that happens to our loved ones.

At the Heart of the Matter

How many times since the death of your loved one have you used the word "should" or "shouldn't" in your self-talk, especially relating to something you wished you had done differently where your loved one was concerned? Under what circumstances are you most likely to use the word "should" today? Take a few minutes to write out your "should" or "shouldn't" statements. If you are working with a group, share your list with the them if you are comfortable doing so.

Now rewrite your "should" statements using the words "choose to" or "chose to" instead of "should".

(Example: Replace "I should have come home earlier from work that day" with "I chose to work over that day. I had no way of knowing what would happen". Or replace "I should be strong for my children" with "I choose to let my children see the reality of how painful this loss is for me".)

_____

_____

_____

_____

_____

_____

_____

_____

_____

_____

_____

Can you feel the difference it makes to choose to stand in strength and take responsibility for your decisions and actions rather than to allow the crippling effect of guilt to rob you of your energy?

Putting It Into Practice

Dealing with the guilt feelings that arise during grief can be a difficult process, one of those "easier said than done" situations. Let's look at some practical strategies for dealing with guilt:

Ask for help.

It's seldom easy to see our own issues clearly. Speaking with someone knowledgeable about the grief process who understands the role that guilt can play can be very helpful in sorting out the legitimate urges to make something right that may really need to be addressed from the ravages of unhealthy guilt.

Make amends where necessary and possible.

If you have hurt someone and are feeling guilty about it, by all means go and make amends. It will free you to forgive yourself. If the person you hurt is the person you lost, you can still make amends. Write a letter to them and read it out loud to a trusted friend, then burn it. Or go to their gravesite and talk out loud to them, telling them what is on your heart. If the person is still living but doesn't want to talk to you, you can make your amends as though they were dead. The amends is as much for you as it is for the other person and this action can still be effective in allowing you to take responsibility for your actions and make a fresh start in your own heart.

Forgive others.

If someone has hurt you, begin the process of moving through the stages of grief in relationship to that particular wound. The moment you make a decision to forgive the other person, you step out of denial and into the next stage in the grief process.

Sometimes resolution comes quickly and sometimes it takes longer. The key is that throughout the forgiveness process, from the anger stage to the acceptance stage, you are committed to loving the person who has hurt you. Your heart is open to healing.

If the wound is deep, you may not be able to be in active relationship with the person (if they are alive) until healthy boundaries have been established. If the person you need to forgive is a loved one who has died, it is still possible to move through the forgiveness process to complete healing. Allow the emotions to surface and face them honestly. Don't shame yourself for any part of the process. Tears, anger, frustration, and confusion are all part of the journey.

Forgive yourself.

Forgiving ourselves is sometimes the hardest part of letting go of unhealthy guilt. Forgiving ourselves means surrendering control and not hanging onto the illusion that there is somehow something we can do to make things okay again. As crazy as it sounds, refusing to forgive ourselves keeps the "ball in our court" and gives us a sense of control.

Create a symbol of finality.

We, as human beings, were created with a need for rituals and symbols. Rituals and symbols give our hearts something concrete to hang onto as a reminder of an important transition in our lives.

Some examples of rituals that might be helpful:

- Write out a list of your unhealthy expectations of yourself and burn it in the presence of a trusted friend.
- Create a memorial fund for your loved one and use it to further a cause he loved.
- Plant a tree in her memory.

A young woman attended a Border Mountain grief workshop several years ago who had lost three family members and her leg in a tragic small aircraft accident. She was experiencing a lot of difficulty grieving the loss because she felt so guilty. She felt, because she had been speaking to the pilot just before the plane crashed, that she had caused the accident. As she processed her grief with the group, she also discovered that she was very angry about not having any part in the decision to amputate her badly injured leg after the accident. She simply woke up with it missing.

With the group's help, this woman created several rituals to help her with letting go of the guilt and anger. She purchased a doll that looked very much like her and asked one group member to act as the doctor and one as the nurse to reenact the hours after the accident.

In the reenactment ceremony, the "doctor" came to her and told her that her leg was badly mangled and asked her permission to remove it. After hearing her "options", she made the decision to let the medical team take the leg. After the "operation", the "nurse" brought the doll's leg to her and respectfully presented it to her. The group followed the woman outside where a small grave had been dug in a peaceful spot in a grove of trees. She read a letter to her leg, grieving the many losses involved in losing it (I miss painting your toes and shaving you...). Then the group helped her bury the leg and gave her flowers and hugs.

The group was able to help her process her deep sense of shame and guilt over distracting the pilot. The group helped her to see that whatever took place behind the controls of the plane was the responsibility of the pilot. He was the one who crashed the plane, not her. To symbolize this realization and create a new body memory around it, the woman fastened a picture of the pilot to a balloon and released it into the air with the group gathered around her for support.

Replace guilt with positive action.

In addition to rituals, there are many "positive action" activities that you can engage in to move your heart along the path to healing. Journaling is a valuable tool, whether it is done in the form of writing or drawing or scrap-booking.

When a young child is upset, parents do "containment" for the child by gently describing the child's emotions for him. "Johnny, I can see that your are angry that Billie took your truck and won't give it back." The child feels heard and understood and is able to face his own emotion with less fear when it is "contained". Journaling is one way to do "containment" for our selves.

Implementing a balanced program of diet and exercise is another helpful "positive action" tool for dealing with the ravages of unhealthy guilt, especially if the exercise is outdoors in a beautiful place. Deep breathing and meditation exercises are also profoundly helpful in releasing unhealthy energy and creating a sense of calm and inner peace.

Develop a long-term support system.

Nothing is more of a deathblow to unhealthy guilt than being a part of good solid support system made up of people who have learned to interact with each other in safe, healthy ways. If you are questioning whether or not your feelings of guilt are cause by a thinking error on your part or if you believe that you have truly wounded someone and may need to make amends, talk to your safe group. Share your feelings and ask them for feedback. Listen as they share their own struggles. Much of what they say will ring true for you, too, and you will feel encouraged, knowing you are not alone in your pain. How can you tell if a group is "safe"? Here are a few characteristics of a safe group:

- Individual members honor confidentiality
- They do not "preach", shame, or give unsolicited advice
- Each member accepts group members unconditionally
- They model acceptance and forgiveness
- Each member is on a healing journey of their own

A Closer Look

Let's take a closer look at a problem that can occur in some groups and with some individuals. It happens when you begin to share with them about the negative emotions and struggles you are having with your grief and they judge, condemn, or explain away your pain with religious answers.

It is called **spiritual abuse** because any time you are emotionally abused by someone in a position of spiritual influence in your life (pastor, priest, rabbi, or other religious leader), you are wounded in two ways: **emotionally** and **spiritually**

Spiritually abusive: Anger is a "sin" and you wouldn't be experiencing it if you were "good enough". (Guilt and shame)
Healthy: Anger is a normal part of the grief process and serves as a "red flag" to alert you to a wound. Anger does not diminish your value in any way.

Spiritually abusive: You don't have enough "faith" if you are still in pain. (Minimizing, shaming)
Healthy: Pain is not a sign of a lack of faith, but a signal that a wound is present. I understand that your wounds will heal as you share your pain with others who love and accept you.

Spiritually abusive: Avoidance and silence. (Neglect, invalidation of your reality)
Healthy: You can state your needs and we, as your safe group, will understand your grief process and provide comfort and support as well as ongoing practical help with the tasks of life that may be too much for you to deal with alone right now (like yard work, caring for young children, or meeting overwhelming financial obligations).

Spiritually abusive: You are given some kind of religious text to read in place of loving support and practical help. (dehumanizing, invalidation of your need)
Healthy: Spiritual principles are demonstrated through loving action.

The human drama
Does not show itself on the surface of life;
It is not played out in the visible world, but in the
hearts of men and women.

Antoine De Saint Exupery

7. Return to the Sunshine
How to Nurture Hope and Find Renewal In the Acceptance Stage of Grief

"Just the facts, please..."

You may have heard it said that one never recovers from grief. This is partly true, in that your life will never be the same as it was before your loss. There is, however, recovery from grief. The sunshine does return. A room in your heart will always be reserved for that special loved one and no one will ever take their place, but once the acceptance stage of grief is reached, life will begin to have meaning again.

Those who have experienced deep grief and have worked through the stages to acceptance have a different outlook on life than those who have never loved and lost. It has been said that grief is the instrument that reams out depths of compassion, understanding, and empathy in the human heart that could never be reached any other way.

In his "Growing Through Loss" workshop, grief counselor Bob Deits speaks of his experience in over 25 years of working with those who have lost loved ones, many in very tragic circumstances. He calls the bereaved "adventurers" because he has found that those who have experienced and conquered grief share more about what they have found than what they have lost.

They are not in denial about the past, but they focus more on the future and what opportunities for growth lay ahead. They possess a deep sense of joy because they have experienced tragedy and survived. They know that there is no curve ball life could throw that will get them down. They are compassionate, patient, and sustain a deep reverence for life and the importance of relationships.

Some questions you may be asking...

 What "mileposts" can I look for to let me know if I have finally reached the acceptance stage of grief?

This stage is rarely reached before the first anniversary of the death, and often isn't reached for many months after that. There won't be distinct and definite signs to let you know you've arrived at "acceptance". Furthermore, at any stage in the grief process, including this one, situations in which we are reminded of the loss can trigger us back to an earlier stage. This is normal and does not mean you are starting all over in your grief process.

Acceptance Stage of Grief

You will know, however, that you are moving into "acceptance" when you feel yourself making a transition from a mindset in which the loss is the central focus of your thoughts and the pivotal point around which everything in your life revolves to one in which "moving on" and "reinvesting" in life is beginning to take precedence.

You may find yourself changing your hairstyle or taking up an interesting new hobby. You might decide to do some traveling that you've never had a chance to do before. You may begin to invest in new relationships or discover new depths in old, familiar ones. Here is what some who have experienced this stage of the grief process have to say:

"I knew healing was happening in my life just recently when I decided to go on a backpacking trip into the mountains that I've wanted to take for years. Throughout my wife's illness, I mostly focused on her needs. Then, after her death, all the processing I had to do to deal with it took up all my energy. I'll always miss her, and I know it will be bittersweet to be there without her, but I'm ready to experience life again. I'm ready to move on."

"It's been three years since my little girl died. It was so hard going through those first days and months. I didn't think I would survive, especially on the anniversary date of the accident. For so long I've been terrified that I would never recover, that I'd never be able to function normally again. Then, I was afraid that I would. That somehow I'd forget how important her life was and how sacred her memory is.

"Now I know that I'll never forget, but I don't have to live every moment in relationship to the loss. This experience has changed me in deep and profound ways. I'm ready to find a way to help others through the nightmare of losing a child. No one should have to do that alone."

 Aren't there some pretty significant differences in how people respond to the grief process? Won't some people take longer to reach the acceptance stage than others?

Yes. Many factors influence how an individual responds to grief. The following are some of the major ones:

• **Cultural framework**

One of the most significant factors influencing the grief response is the culture in which the person was raised. "Socially acceptable" grief responses can vary significantly from culture to culture. Some cultures are very emotionally expressive, while others tend to avoid any overt show of feelings. Often, the cultures that do not express feelings overtly tend to rely on rich ceremony and symbolism to express grief.

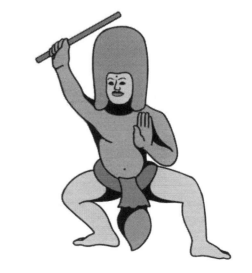

- ## Family rules of expression

As we learned in Chapter 2, family systems influence the emotional expression of individual family members to a great extent. Some families encourage emotional support between members and others suppress it. In a closed family system, any admission of fear or "negative" emotion is unacceptable. This suppression of emotion retards the grief process and can prevent healing altogether.

- ## Relationship with the deceased

The closer the relationship to the one who died, the more intensely the bereaved will sense the loss. This is especially true in the face of closely intertwined experience, dreams, goals, and future plans.

A stressful relationship, in which communication was unhealthy and a high level of dependency was present, will also create a setting for intense grief. Unresolved family issues can exacerbate guilt and prolong the grief process.

- ## Circumstances of the death

An expected death, with hospice involved to help family members work through the anticipatory grief process, is less likely to precipitate an unhealthy grief reaction than a sudden death by suicide or homicide. The death of an older person who has voiced a readiness to die is usually easier to accept than the death of a child who hasn't had a chance to "live" yet.

- ## Religious beliefs

The bereaved person's spiritual support system has a tremendous impact on her ability to cope with the wrenching pain of separation from a loved one in death. Several studies have shown that religious rituals aid in the emotional healing process.

• Personal coping skills

Whenever a crisis occurs in an individual's life, they fall back on the coping skills they have developed from early childhood on to adulthood. If their coping skills are based in shame and unhealthy beliefs about themselves, the grieving process will be much more painful and much more likely to develop into abnormal grief.

Pre-existing bio-chemical challenges such as clinical depression, bi-polar disorder, or seasonal affective disorder sets an individual up for complications in the grief process.

If you suffer from any kind of brain chemistry issues, make absolutely certain that you have careful oversight of your physical care by a physician who understands both the grief process and your unique needs relative to it. If you don't feel "heard" or your physician seems inattentive to your concerns, find another physician.

• Personality of the individual

Some personalities are naturally more introspective and serious, investing every event in life with personal meaning. Others are more outgoing and

surface in their relationships and tend to heal more quickly from wounds and move on with life. No certain personality type is "good" and "right" any more than any of them are "bad" or "wrong". They are just different and different is normal.

• Current life stress

Stress is cumulative. Some major stressors are death, divorce, moving, having a baby, changing jobs, experiencing a natural disaster, and others. If there are several major stressors already depleting your energy, this major loss has the potential to push you over the brink in your coping ability if you don't actively seek the support you need to get through it.

- ## Physical health

A person's health can have a huge impact on their ability to cope with added stressors in their life. A handicap or physical ailment can short-circuit one of the most important stress relievers available to the bereaved: regular outdoor exercise. If you are dealing with health issues in conjunction with your grief process you will need to be extra attentive to your physical needs and ask for help (if you need it) in getting outside on a regular basis.

- ## Support System

Loving support is crucial to a person coping with the pain of losing a loved one. Those who, before the crisis occurred, established a healthy support network of friends and family cope far more healthfully with the grief process in all its painful phases than someone who has built a life based on isolation.

At the Heart of the Matter

Take a few moments to look deep within your heart as you review your experience with grief thus far. What are the gifts your grief has given you that you could never have received any other way? In what ways has your grief changed you? If you feel comfortable doing so, share your answers with the group if you are working with one.

_____

_____

_____

_____

_____

_____

_____

_____

_____

_____

_____

_____

_____

_____

_____

_____

_____

_____

There will never be
another now,
I'll make the most of today.

There will never be
another me,
I'll make the most of myself.

Anonymous

Putting it Into Practice

Moving into the acceptance stage of grief can be a frightening journey in and of itself as the disarray that comes with deep loss gives way to a new life. Who am I now that I have survived this wound? Who will I be as I move into new, uncharted territory? Old roles are forever gone. What will the new ones look like?

Let's look at some guidelines for easing this transition and optimizing growth:

1. Allow humor to do its work.

Edgar N. Jackson, in his book *The Many Faces of Grief*, describes humor as "psychic lubricant". We laugh at what we fear. Somehow those mystery-filled areas of life and those anxiety-creating events lose their terror in the face of humor. Humor targets a problem and "takes it down a peg". This makes it less frightening to look at later, when we are ready to tackle it seriously.

The many changes that loss brings into our lives can trigger a high level of anxiety that can cause us to tense up. Grief itself produces a lot of nervous tension that settles in the joints and connective tissue. Laughing relaxes the skeletal system, especially the lower jaw, where a lot of nervous tension is stored. It also relaxes the diaphragm, improving the flow of oxygen to the heart and internal organs. A deep "belly laugh" is as therapeutic as a "good cry", as both result in the release of nervous tension.

Laughing won't be disrespectful to the memory of your loved one, although it may feel at first as if it is. If guilt feelings arise as you let yourself laugh, deal with them directly in your journal and with your safe group. When you have found the root of your feelings, then they will no longer rule your decisions. Then, rent a funny movie and laugh!

2. Watch your nutrition

We are holistic beings and whatever affects us emotionally will affect us physically and spiritually and vice versa. The way we nourish (or deplete) our bodies nutritionally will have a direct impact on how we handle grief. Caffeine drinks, sugary foods, alcohol, and fried foods deplete our body's resources and make it more difficult for us to handle any stress, especially the heavy stress of grief.

It is easier on the body to eat several small meals in a day than to skip meals and make up for them in one big meal. Blood sugar fluctuations can trigger depression. Control blood sugar levels by eating regular, nutritionally balanced meals.

Resist the temptation to munch on highly processed snack foods. Eating is a comforting activity as much of our society associates mealtime with emotional connection. Too much snack food will fill you up with empty calories and create a nutritional imbalance in your body, leaving you susceptable to fatigue and depression.

Eat more protein (eggs, nuts, nut butters, seeds) than carbohydrates in the morning to give you energy. Eat more carbohydrates (beans, whole grain pastas, brown rice) than protein in the evening to relax you in preparation for sleep. Aim for making fresh fruits and vegetables as close to 80% of your diet as you can.

Find a good nutritional supplement company and take their line of vitamins and minerals faithfully. It is better to stick with one company that you trust than to take different vitamins and minerals from here and there that have not been formulated to work together optimally. In addition to a good vitamin and mineral supplement, consider taking a concentrated grape seed or pine bark extract (to fight free radical damage caused by stress), plenty of calcium, and an oil blend that contains Omega 3 essential fatty acids (crucial "brain food"). Other helpful supplements are gingko biloba, barley grass powder, and glutamine (always check with your physician before starting any kind of supplement).

3. Drink at least 8-10 glasses of water daily

Studies have shown that people experiencing grief tend toward dehydration. Do your body a favor and leave off the beverages that dehydrate you further (alcohol, coffee, tea, and soda). Instead drink plenty of fresh, clean water, spaced out in regular intervals during the day, to prevent the lethargy, confusion, constipation, electrolyte imbalances, and build-up of toxic waste that dehydration causes in your body.

4. Get plenty of exercise in the great outdoors

Outdoor exercise is the best way to release those brain chemicals called endorphins that greatly increase our sense of well being and can dramatically improve mood. Try to get at least a 30 minute brisk walk scheduled into every day, an hour is even better. Check with your doctor before initiating any new exercise program.

Bicycling, swimming, tennis, golf, jogging, canoeing, kayaking, in-line skating, backpacking, and horseback riding are all great supplemental activities that will keep your muscles toned and your outlook on life positive. It can be a powerful mood enhancer to paddle through a wildlife refuge in the quiet of the morning in your cedar strip canoe!

"But I can't afford to take the time off work for such a thing," you may say. My answer is, "Can you really afford *not* to?"

5. Rest

Some people need only five or six hours of sleep each night. Others, especially those highly sensitive people who experience everything in life more acutely, need eight or nine hours of sleep per night to allow their bodies to recharge and rebuild. Make sure you are getting the amount of sleep your body needs. If you are shortchanging yourself in the sleep department, you may experience irritability, difficulty concentrating, and a low tolerance from frustration during your waking hours.

6. Connect with others regularly

Isolation is deadly. The story is told of a Russian orphanage where some babies thrived and others died even though all were receiving adequate nutrition. It was discovered that the babies that thrived were in a ward where a loving and nurturing nurse held and rocked each baby on a regular basis. The babies that died were not held, touched or spoken to. Essentially, those babies died for lack of human contact.

The need for human contact does not end in infancy. We were all created with the need for contact with others. We need to be touched and to touch. We need to be able to express our emotions and be understood. We need to speak our hearts and be heard. Make sure that your support system is well established and broad enough to meet your needs.

Tips for Getting Better Rest

- Try warm milk or soothing herb tea before going to bed.

- Establish a routine of going to bed at the same time each night and getting up at the same time every morning.

- Lying down while you watch a boring television program or reading a book with lots of relaxing descriptions of scenery (i.e. Michener's historical novels) may help you nod off.

- Avoid naps in the daytime, even if you feel very sleepy then. Take a walk until the urge to catnap passes.

- Avoid stimulants such as coffee, caffeinated tea, chocolate, and soft drinks that contain caffeine.

- A hot bath before retiring can be very relaxing, especially if you add some aroma therapy products designed to enhance a restful state of mind.

- Eat a light meal in the evening instead of a heavy one, and don't eat after seven pm.

- Adjust the temperature in your sleeping room to help you sleep most comfortably. Cooler air in the bedroom may be more comfortable as long as the air is not too dry.

- If it is fear that is keeping you awake at night, do whatever it takes to relieve your fears. Install an alarm system, get a dog, lock your bedroom door, leave a light on, etc.

- Try listening to relaxing music.

- If sleeping in your bed is a painful reminder that your spouse is no longer with you, try sleeping on his side of the bed and using his pillow. It is easier to cope with seeing your side of the bed empty.

- Don't try to make yourself go to sleep. If none of the usual relaxation enhancers work, get up and do something else for awhile then start the bedtime routine again.

 # A Closer Look

Let's take a closer look at some ways to tell if you are moving into the acceptance stage of grief and coming to a place of healing. If your loss is new, familiarize yourself with the concepts here, then refer back to this list later as you have had a chance to move through the earlier stages of grief. Even if you feel you are in the acceptance stage of grief, don't worry if you don't have all the signs of healing yet. Moving through grief is a gradual process and each person's heart has a healing timetable all its own.

Signs of Healing

- **Able to enjoy time alone**

- **Actually looking forward to holidays**

- **Enjoyment of a joke**

- **Eating, sleeping, and exercise patterns return to "normal"**

- **A renewed sense of energy and purpose**

- **A routine develops in daily life**

- **Able to concentrate on a book or favorite TV program**

- Can review both "good" and "bad" memories

- Able to drive somewhere alone without crying

- Can sit through a religious service without crying

- Establishing new and healthy relationships

- Organizing and planning for the future

- Looking forward to getting up in the morning

- Reinvesting the energy once spent on the deceased in other projects

- Enjoying life's pleasant experiences

- No longer needing daily or weekly trips to the cemetery

- Acceptance of things as they are instead of trying to return to how they were

- Treating your grief "attacks" with patience

- Able to discover personal growth from the grief process

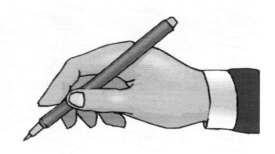

Another important topic to look at when discussing grief is the grief process that children go through relative to loss. In our own pain, we sometimes overlook the impact the loss is having on our children or grandchildren. The following guidelines briefly define some of the ways children react to loss. It is meant as a brief overview and does not take the place of working with a skilled children's counselor or family therapist to give the children a chance to speak their pain and work through their fears in their own way.

A Child's Grief

When the person who died or left is one of the child's care providers, the child will most likely react in four basic ways:

Fear
Fear that she will lose the other parent or that she, too, will die can cause the child to react in an insecure, clingy manner. Other fears include a fear of going to sleep, of being separated from close family members, or of being unprotected. On top of all these fears, she will likely be afraid to share her feelings with others.

Guilt
There are many things that children tend to feel guilty about when a parent dies. Guilt can rise from anything at all, so it is sometimes hard to identify the source. There are, however, some basic beliefs that are common to children who have lost parents.

One common belief that causes tremendous guilt in the child is that the death is a punishment for their misbehaving. Children at certain developmental stages are very concrete in their thinking and reason from cause to effect in a direct and deliberate way. If something goes wrong, they easily assume they are to blame.

Believing that the parent died because they willed it so, or that they didn't love the parent enough to prevent the death, or that it isn't right for them to be alive when the parent is dead can all cause a heavy load of guilt in the child.

Anger

A child whose parent has died is likely to start misbehaving and acting in very aggressive ways at school and at home. The anger that spawns such behavior is often rooted in the child's underlying belief that he has been abandoned. He also may feel that his is unimportant and that his future has been taken away from him. He may feel that he is fighting forces so much bigger than himself that he has no chance of "winning" and be furious at how unfair it all seems.

Confusion

In a situation that would bewilder even the most self-possessed adult, imagine the confusion that a child must feel when she has just had her world turned upside down by the death of a parent. Trying to sort out the overwhelming feelings triggered by such a traumatic event is a daunting task for the child, and she probably hasn't had the chance to develop her communications skills to the point of ever being able to describe how she feels.

The grieving child will likely be confused about other's expectations of her, about her own emotional reactions, and about her perceptions and memories of the deceased parent's life and death.

Telling a Child About a Death

It is crucial when telling a child about a death that has occurred, whether it be a parent, sibling, grandparent, or other family member or friend, that the person breaking the news be sensitive and aware of the child's needs.

- **Tell the truth about the death**

- **Use simple and easy to understand language**

- **Be direct (no euphemisms)**

- **Lay the groundwork for future explanations when the child is older**

- **Let the child know they will be involved in rituals surrounding the death (funeral, memorial service, etc.)**

- **Assure the child that their feelings are accepted**

How to Help a Grieving Child Heal

- Don't act as if the parent or loved one did not die

- Encourage the child to express feelings

- Share your memories and feelings about the one who died with the child

- Be affectionate with the child, emotionally and physically

- Reassure the child that his basic needs will be met

- Help the child plan for the future

- Encourage open and honest communication within the family

- Help the child deal with feelings of anger, depression, and bewilderment

- Explore and address the child's feelings of guilt

- Encourage the family to participate in family therapy

When an Adult Child Loses a Parent

- They may be losing a friend, advisor, and consultant as well as a parent

- There is often a sense of losing part of one's family history and roots

- There can be a significant sense of loss of support and unconditional love

- Conflicts and ambivalent feelings about the past may be stirred up

- Family roles and responsibilities may change

- The grieving adult child may be expected to "get over" the loss more quickly than if it were a spouse who died

- It can be a strong reminder of one's own mortality

Thank you for sharing this part of your journey through grief with me. May you be richly blessed as you discover new depths of healing in the days to come. It is a difficult road and you are more than a survivor. **You are a champion**

"For he has given laughter in my sadness
and colored rainbows with my pain."

Shelly Chapin

May the road rise to meet you.
May the wind be always at your back.
May the sun shine warm upon your face.
And rains fall soft upon your fields.
And until we meet again,
May God hold you in the hollow of His hand.

Old Irish Blessing

Appendix A

Mindfulness Exercise/Meditation
Vonda L. Winkle

Exercise One

Sit in an open, relaxed position with your feet flat on the floor and your hands open with palms up or palms down. If working with a group, your leader will advise when to start and stop the exercise. If working on your own, you may wish to set a timer for several minutes (or longer as you practice these techniques and discover which ones are most helpful for you and how long each exercise is comfortable to perform) , When prompted by your group leader, or when you are ready to start, close your eyes and breath naturally. Take a deep breath in through your nose and then out through your mouth, pursing your lips to create a little resistance. Do this slowly and mindfully nine more times. Once you reach the count of ten, start over with one until your leader or timer ends the execise. Slowly open your eyes and come back into the room.

Exercise Two

This exercise is the same as the first one, however this time, as you maintain a relaxed position, "push" everything you are holding on to out of your body with each count.

Take 3-5 minutes at this point to divide into small groups of 2 or 3. Share your experience with your partner or small group. Which exercise was more effective in helping you to relax? Why?

Exercise Three

Maintain the same posture as in the first two exercises. Visualize yourself hiking along a trail in the forest. There is a creek to your left and lush vegetation—ferns, fir trees, and forest greenery—surrounds you. You approach a large log that lays across the creek beside the trail and you leave the trail for a moment to rest on the log and listen to the rushing sound of the creek tumbling over rocks. The trees above you gently sway in the wind and you pick up the scent of pine needles and damp earth under your feet.

You stand up after awhile and cross a small bridge. The creek is now on your right and you begin to hear the distant sound of a waterfall. The vegetation thickens around you as the sound of the water falling rises to a muffled roar.

Suddenly you find yourself in an opening in the forest and just before you is a magnificent waterfall. The pounding of the water hitting the pool below it is so loud it drowns out all other noise. You continue standing and watching the water fall from the top, tumbling into the pool below. Then, when your leader or timer signals the end of your session, slowly open your eyes and gently come back into your room.

Exercise Four

Begin this exercise in the same way as the others. Visualize yourself at the top of a long spiral staircase. Turn on a light if you need one to help you see your way, then slowly start down the stairs, using the rail to help guide you. Wind down the stairs for awhile, then sit down on one of the steps to rest for a bit. Bring yourself to your feet and continue down the stairs. Keep winding your way down until you reach the bottom, then sit in silence until your leader or timer ends the exercise.

Discuss your experience with the group. Did you find one exercise more difficult than the others? Why? What responses did you observe in yourself?

Choose one of the exercises to use for daily relaxation. Do not go back and forth between exercises but stick with the one that is the most effective for you. Use the exercise daily to maintain mindfulness and relaxation.

Made in the USA
San Bernardino, CA
24 September 2018